FORMED IN CHRIST SERIES

ABOUT THE SERIES

Who is Jesus Christ? What does it mean to know him? What do the Church and her sacraments have to do with him? How are we to follow him?

These are the questions at the heart of the Catholic faith, and these are the questions the Formed in Christ series answers. Rooted in the story of Salvation History and steeped in the writings of the Fathers and Doctors of the Church, this series of high school textbooks from the St. Paul Center seeks to engage minds and hearts as it presents the tenets of the Catholic faith in Scripture and Tradition.

Over the course of this comprehensive, four-year curriculum, students will learn the fundamentals of Church teaching on the Person and mission of Jesus Christ, Sacred Scripture, the Church, the sacraments, morality, Church history, vocations, Catholic social teaching, and more. Just as important, they'll be invited, again and again, to enter more deeply into a relationship with Christ, growing in love of him as they grow in knowledge of him.

PUBLISHED

Evidence of Things Unseen: An Introduction to Fundamental Theology
Andrew Willard Jones and Louis St. Hilaire.
Edited by Emily Stimpson Chapman

The Word Became Flesh: An Introduction to Christology
Andrew Willard Jones. Edited by Emily Stimpson Chapman

That You Might Have Life: An Introduction to the Paschal Mystery of Christ
Louis St. Hilaire. Edited by Emily Stimpson Chapman

I Will Build My Church: An Introduction to Ecclesiology
Andrew Willard Jones. Edited by Emily Stimpson Chapman

Do This in Remembrance: An Introduction to the Sacraments
Jacob Wood. Edited by Emily Stimpson Chapman

Christ Alive in Us: An Introduction to Moral Theology
John Meinert and Emily Stimpson Chapman

D1559422

THE WORD OF TRUTH

AN INTRODUCTION TO SACRED SCRIPTURE

THE WORD OF TRUTH

AN INTRODUCTION TO SACRED SCRIPTURE

EMILY STIMPSON CHAPMAN

TAN Books &
Emmaus Road Publishing

In Grateful Recognition of Lawrence Joseph & Lynn Marie Blanford

Unless otherwise noted, Scripture quotations are taken from The Revised Standard Version Second Catholic Edition (Ignatius Edition) Copyright © 2006 by the Division of Christian Education of the National Council of the Churches of Christ in the United States of America. Used by permission. All rights reserved.

Excerpts from the *Catechism of the Catholic Church*, second edition, copyright © 2000, Libreria Editrice Vaticana--United States Conference of Catholic Bishops, Washington, D.C. Noted as "CCC" in the text.

Cover image: Sermon on the Mount, 1877, Carl Bloch. Restored Traditions.

Series design by Margaret Ryland

ISBN 978-1-5051-2064-6

Emmaus Road Publishing
1468 Parkview Circle
Steubenville, Ohio 43952

TAN Books
PO Box 269
Gastonia, NC 28053

Printed in the United States of America

TABLE OF CONTENTS

Part I

Divine Revelation— God Speaks to Us

Walk into a library—any library, anywhere in the world. Survey the books before you. Count them. Look at their authors, their titles, their topics. Each, in some way, has the power to change you. Some will inspire you. Some will teach you. Some will harm you. But no book you see—not a single one—will change you as much as Sacred Scripture.

St. Paul explains, "All Scripture is inspired by God and profitable for teaching, for reproof, for correction, and for training in righteousness, that the man of God may be complete, equipped for every good work" (2 Tim 3:16–17).

There are, of course, plenty of other books out there that will teach you, correct you, and train you in "righteousness"—that is, help you to become a good and just person. But not one of those other books will do it so well as Sacred Scripture, because not one of those other books is inspired by God. No other book is the Word of God. Moreover, not one of those books will, in St. Paul's words, "complete" you, because not one of those books will bring you into a direct, personal encounter with the Word of God made flesh: Jesus Christ.

Nothing else you ever read will be as important as Sacred Scripture. This is why it's so important that you read it correctly. The Holy Bible isn't like other books. If you just pick it up and try reading it cover to cover, from beginning to end, it's easy to get confused. It's easy to lose the thread of the biblical "plot." It's easy to miss the point of it all.

The reason for the book you're holding is to help you not miss the point. During this course, this book will help answer some of your most fundamental questions about the Holy Bible: What is Scripture? How is it inspired by God? Why do we have the Bible? Why should we read it? How should we interpret it? Why does it matter to me?

As the answers to these questions emerge, you'll learn to navigate the Holy Bible with greater confidence and knowledge. You'll also see the scope of Salvation History—God's saving work in time—and understand your place in that history. Most importantly, you'll have the opportunity to grow closer to Jesus by spending time prayerfully contemplating God's Word.

Chapter 1

God's Self-Revelation in Words, Deeds, and Covenants

God made you, God loves you, and God wants to be in a relationship with you—now and eternally. We were made to know this. We were made to know God. "The desire for God is written in the human heart . . . and God never ceases to draw man to himself," says the Catechism (27). How does God do that, though? How does God teach us about himself, helping us to know him and love him in return?

The natural world is where he starts. Like a book written in the voice of its author or a painting that bears the brushstrokes of the artist who made it, everything in creation bears the mark of its Creator. Signs of God's goodness and love, his power and majesty, his providence and care are everywhere. Simply by looking at the world around us, we can know a great deal about God; evidence of who he is and how he loves us is in every sunset and mountaintop, every flower and grain of wheat.

While the natural world reveals much about God to us, it doesn't reveal everything. There are some truths about God's nature and God's plan that we can't perceive on our own power. Nature isn't enough. It isn't sufficient. For some truths, more is needed. This "more" comes to us through divine Revelation. Through divine Revelation, God shows us both himself and his plan for us.

The fullness of divine Revelation—the way that God has most perfectly shown himself to us—is "by sending us his beloved Son, our Lord Jesus Christ, and the Holy Spirit" (CCC 50). Through Jesus, we can know who God is. "He who has seen me has seen the Father," Jesus tells us (John 14:9). Likewise, through Jesus we have access to God and can share in his divine nature (CCC 51). As adopted sons and daughters of God, in Christ we have the opportunity to respond to God, know God, and love God beyond what we could do on our own (CCC 52).

At the same time, while Jesus Christ is God's perfect self-revelation, God didn't simply reveal all of himself at once in Palestine in the first century and expect humanity to see and understand everything immediately. Rather, God communicated himself to us "gradually" (CCC 53) by his deeds and words, through stages of revelation that we call Salvation History.

An Overview of Salvation History

Salvation History is the true story of how God revealed himself to humanity in time—helping us to know him, trust him, and love him—so that he could bring about the divine plan of our salvation through "the person and mission of the incarnate Word, Jesus Christ" (CCC 53). Salvation History is, in a sense, the plot of the Bible.

This plot unfolds through a series of covenants with mankind, with each covenant bringing more and more people into the family of God. Before we look at each of these covenants in detail, however, it's important to understand what a covenant is.

Unlike contracts, which involve the exchange of goods and services, covenants involve the exchange of persons. Marriage is one example of a covenant. In marriage, a man and woman give themselves completely to one another. Adoption is another form of a covenant. In adoption, a child receives parents as his own, and a man and woman receive a child as their own.

In the ancient world, covenants were typically made with an oath and sealed through a liturgical ritual and meal. Likewise, covenants always came with terms (often called the "covenant law"). People would give themselves to one another, but under certain conditions. In biblical times, if those conditions weren't met, some kind of punishment (for example, death) followed. If the conditions were fulfilled, blessing followed.

Covenants were, generally speaking, quite common in ancient societies. Most of these covenants, however, were made between two people or groups of people, not with God. The people of Israel, though, were different. They were the only ancient nation that even believed themselves to have entered into covenants with God himself, let alone actually did.

The Covenants of the Old Testament

The first of these covenants is recounted in the Book of Genesis. There, God creates man and woman "in his own image" (Gen 1:27) He shares his very life with Adam and Eve and allows them to know him intimately. All Adam and Eve had to do to honor this covenant was obey the one condition God gave them: to not eat of the tree of the knowledge of good and evil (Gen 2:15–17). But Adam and Eve disobeyed God, and sin entered the world. This original sin merited Adam, Eve, and all their descendants the punishment of death—both physical death and spiritual death. After our first parents fell, the gates to heaven were closed to us. Because of God's love, however, he promised to one day send a savior—a redeemer—who would open those gates once more (CCC 55).

God's first covenant was with a married couple: Adam and Eve. His next covenant was with a family: the family of Noah. After destroying much of a sinful world with a great flood, God made a new covenant with Noah and his sons (Gen 9). He gave them a new law to obey and, in turn, promised that he would never destroy the world in such a way again. The account of this covenant uses language that is reminiscent of the creation account and implies a type of renewal of creation, a restoration of the original peace (*shalom* in Hebrew) harmed through sin.

Unfortunately, Noah's descendants did little better than their ancestors. They began committing terrible sins and eventually attempted to build a great tower in the city of Babel, rejecting God's sovereignty in the process. God punished them by destroying the tower, scattering the people, and confusing their language. In time, though, God reached out to another man, Abram (whose name God later changed to Abraham).

With Abram and his tribe, or extended family, God would make a new covenant. But first, God called Abram to leave his homeland. If Abram obeyed, God promised to bless him in three ways: (1) by granting him many descendants; (2) by making his name "great"; and (3) by blessing all the nations through his descendants (Gen 12). These three promises are "upgraded" into covenants in Genesis 15, 17, and 22.

Centuries later, God worked through Moses to expand his covenant family even further. After leading the descendants of Abraham, Isaac, and Jacob out of slavery in Israel, he called an entire nation—the nation of Israel—to be his people. He promised to make them a nation of kings and high priests who would teach the world to walk in God's ways, and gave them a new, more detailed covenant law to obey—a law that included the Ten Commandments.

Although the people of Israel repeatedly broke the terms of their covenant with God—forcing God to give them increasingly specific and "lower" laws to obey—Israel eventually grew into a great kingdom. Through God's covenant with their king, David, not only Israel but also the Gentiles (non-Israelites) were brought into the covenant, although not as full participants.

Waiting for Fulfillment

The years that passed between God's covenant with Adam and God's covenant with David were all marked by a similar pattern. God called someone out as the covenant mediator (Adam, Noah, Abraham, Moses, and David). He gave them the terms of the covenant (the covenant law) and, for a time, the people lived in accord with those terms. Then they sinned, meriting the same punishment as Adam and Eve: death. More time would pass, and God would reach out again, including an ever-expanding group of people in the covenant, moving from a couple, to a family, to a tribe, to a nation, and then to a kingdom. And yet, the pattern kept repeating itself. No matter how hard they tried, humanity couldn't live up to what God asked of them. Which meant they couldn't receive the fullness of the blessings promised to them.

At the same time, God's covenant promises were going unfulfilled. No redeemer came to crush the head of the serpent. No descendant of Abraham's blessed all nations. Israel had not become a holy nation of priests, leading the world to God. And the Kingdom of David, which God had said would last forever, was destroyed by the Assyrians and Babylonians.

Something more was needed. Something more had to happen. That something, the prophets promised, was a New Covenant, with which God would fulfill his plan to make all men and women part of his covenant family. As the prophet Jeremiah foretold, "the days are coming, says the LORD, when I will make a new covenant with the house of Israel and the house of Judah. . . . I will be their God, and they shall be my people" (see Jer 31:31–34; 32:36–41).

God's Final Covenant

These covenants between Israel and God were part of divine Revelation. They were God revealing himself to his chosen people over time in human terms: family, land, kings, the passage of time itself. Theologians speak of this behavior as "divine condescension." This means God was meeting us at our level, putting lofty truths into lowly language that we could understand. Like a teacher who gradually introduces more challenging concepts to students as they learn and grow, God was gradually giving Israel deeper insights into his nature as they matured as a people.

All of this was meant to prepare Israel for God's final and definitive self-revelation, Jesus Christ, the Word made flesh. Through calling people out, making himself known, and giving them laws to obey, God was forming his people. He was teaching them about himself, about themselves, and about how they were made to live, so they could receive the fullness of Revelation himself: Jesus Christ.

Through Jesus' physical presence among us, through his words and deeds, his signs and wonders (see Rom 15:18–19), and, above all, through his suffering, death, Resurrection, and sending of the Spirit,

Jesus made God known to the world. He—the Word of God—is God's final word on himself: "In him he has said everything; there will be no other word than this one" (CCC 65).

Moreover, through his life and death, Jesus finally and perfectly fulfilled all the promises of the old covenants. He was the redeemer promised to Adam. He brought about a true new creation, as promised to Noah. He is the descendant of Abraham, who blesses all nations. He is the new Moses, who leads people out of sin and into the promised land of eternal life. He also makes his people into a kingdom of priests, all of whom, in Christ, can offer life-giving sacrifices. Lastly, he is the Son of David, who reigns eternally over the kingdom of God.

The Incarnation really was the goal to which the whole history of salvation was building. Through his life and ministry, Jesus made God known to us. And through his suffering, death, and Resurrection—known as the Paschal Mystery—Jesus both fulfilled the promises of the Old Covenant and instituted a New Covenant. He announced this New Covenant the night before he died, at the Last Supper, saying, "This cup which is poured out for you is the new covenant in my blood" (Luke 22:20).

The New Covenant, like the Old, has *conditions*: we must believe in Jesus, be baptized, eat and drink his Flesh and Blood in the Eucharist, and live according to the commands he gave. Those commands—to love God with all your heart, mind, soul, and strength, and to love one another as Christ loves us—are the cornerstone of the New Covenant law. The Eucharist is the ongoing liturgy of the New Covenant. And, as the culmination of all the earlier covenants, this New Covenant has the widest reach; it invites not just a couple, a family, a tribe, a nation, or a kingdom to be part of God's family—it invites the entire world. The final form God's family takes is a universal (catholic, or *katholicos* in Greek) kingdom, which Jesus calls his Church.

In the Mass, the Eucharistic Prayer IV summarizes these stages of revelation:

> You formed man in your own image
> and entrusted the whole world to his care,

so that in serving you alone, the Creator,

he might have dominion over all creatures.

And when through disobedience he had lost your friendship,

you did not abandon him to the domain of death.

For you came in mercy to the aid of all,

so that those who seek might find you.

Time and again you offered them covenants

and through the prophets

taught them to look forward to salvation.

And you so loved the world, Father most holy,

that in the fullness of time

you sent your Only Begotten Son to be our Savior.[1]

The blessings of the New Covenant exceed anything that had been imagined in the Old. God sent us his Son and the Holy Spirit (CCC 50) so that we might become sons in the Son. Or, as St. Athanasius put it, "The Son of God became the Son of Man so that sons of men could become sons of God."[2]

Even more amazingly, God made the sign of the New Covenant the Eucharist. In the Eucharist, the God of the Universe takes on the appearance of bread and wine and gives himself to us in a real, physical way. And when we receive him reverently and worthily, we give ourselves back to him. The Eucharist is truly Holy Communion—it is a holy communion between God and us.

All this is to say that the goal of God's whole plan of revelation—the end of the whole sweep of Salvation History—was to bring us into the closest, most loving, most intimate relationship possible with him. In other words, Salvation History, in its deepest essence, is a love story; it's the story of God's love for us.

---

[1] *The Roman Missal*, trans. The International Commission on English in the Liturgy, 3rd typical ed. (Washington, DC: United States Conference of Catholic Bishops, 2011), no. 117.

[2] Athanasius, quoted in Scott Hahn, "The Mystery of the Family of God," in *Catholic for a Reason: Scripture and the Mystery of the Family of God* (Steubenville, OH: Emmaus Road, 2000), 13.

SELECTED READING:
Scott Hahn, "The Mystery of the Family of God," *Catholic for a Reason: Scripture and the Mystery of the Family of God*, pp. 11–13

Let us consider four doctrinal areas in order to see how this Trinitarian familial perspective may enhance our understanding:

1. Creator and Creation: Seeing creation as the work of the Trinity enables us to see the world differently. God is more than our Creator; He is Our Father by grace. Instead of mere creatures, we are made in God's image and likeness to live as His sons and daughters. Instead of a vast impersonal cosmos, the Father fashioned the world to be our home—a royal palace and a holy temple.

2. Covenant and Law: More than a legal contract, a covenant is a sacred family bond. So God's covenants in salvation history (with Adam, Noah, Abram, Moses, David, and Jesus) reveal how He fathers His ever-expanding family and maintains its unity and solidarity. Accordingly, the laws of the covenant are not arbitrary stipulations forcefully imposed by a superior power, but rather expressions of God's fatherly wisdom, goodness, and love. We obey them in order to mature, so that we can love like God.

When God makes and keeps covenants with His people, He's just being true to Himself—for the Trinity is a covenantal Being.

"Covenant" is *what* God does because "covenant" is *who* God is.

3. Sin and Judgment: More than broken laws, sin means broken lives and broken homes. At root, sin comes from our refusal to keep the covenant, so we lose the grace of divine sonship. We sin because we don't want to love as much as God loves us; it's too demanding. Sin is absurd and deadly—for in sinning, we stupidly prefer something other than the life and love to which Our Father calls us. God punishes sin with death because sin is what kills His life in us. Judgment is not an impersonal legal process, nor are the covenant curses enactments of God's vindictive wrath. Like God's covenant law, the curses are not expressions of hatred, but fatherly love and discipline; they impose suffering that is remedial, restorative, and redemptive. God's wrath is not opposed to His love; it's an expression of it. God *is* love (1 Jn. 4:8), but His love is a consuming fire (Heb. 12:29). That fiery love reflects the inner life of the Trinity. Sinners don't escape God's love; they get burned by it—unless and until they reopen themselves to it. That is what repentance achieves, and that's what God's wrath is for. Seeing God as Father doesn't lessen the severity of His wrath, nor is a lower standard of justice implied. On the contrary, a good father requires more from his sons and daughters than judges from defendants. And a good father also shows greater mercy.

4. Salvation and the Church: Salvation is not only *from* sin, but *for* sonship—in Christ. We are not only forgiven by God's grace, we are adopted and divinized, that is, we "become partakers of the divine nature" (2 Pet. 1:4). This is ultimately why God created us, to share in the life-giving love of the Trinity. Self-sacrificial love is the essential law of God's covenant, which we broke—but Jesus kept. After assuming our humanity, He transformed it into a perfect image—and instrument—of the Trinity's love, by offering it as a sacrificial gift-of-self to the Father on our behalf. The Son of God "took the form of a servant" (Phil. 2:6) so that sinful servants may be restored as sons of God. As Saint Athanasius declared: "The Son of God became the Son of Man so that sons of men could become sons of God."

By establishing the New Covenant, Christ founded one Church—through His own resurrected body—as an extension of His Incarnation and the Trinity's life. The Catholic Church is the universal Family of God, outside of which there is no salvation. This teaching does not condemn anyone. Rather, it simply clarifies the essential meaning of salvation and the Church. Since the essence of salvation is the life of divine sonship, to speak of salvation outside of God's family, the Church, is to confuse things greatly—since being *outside* God's family is precisely what we need to be saved from (see Catechism, nos. 845–48).

QUESTIONS FOR REVIEW

1. What is divine Revelation?
2. What is a covenant?
3. Name the mediators of the covenants in the Old Testament.
4. Who is the fullness of divine Revelation?
5. How did Jesus fulfill the covenants of the Old Testament?

QUESTIONS FOR DISCUSSION

1. What evidence of God's love for you have you seen in the world around you and your own life?
2. What does God's gradual revelation of himself in history tell you about him and his love for humanity?
3. How has God revealed himself to you? How have you come to know him better through the years?

Chapter 2

THE TRANSMISSION OF DIVINE
REVELATION

When the Son of God became man, he made the truth of who he was known through both his words and deeds. He told parables, preached sermons on mountaintops, and answered the questions of Jewish leaders. He also healed the sick, resurrected the dead, and multiplied loaves and fish. Then, after his Resurrection, shortly before he returned to the Father in heaven and sent the Holy Spirit to us, he told his Apostles to do the same:

> Go therefore and make disciples of all nations, baptizing them in the name of the Father and of the Son and of the Holy Spirit, teaching them to observe all that I have commanded you; and behold, I am with you always, to the close of the age. (Matt 28:19–20)

This final command of the Lord before his Ascension into heaven is known as the Great Commission. After Pentecost, filled with the Holy Spirit, the Apostles responded to this commission by transmitting the Gospel in three ways: orally, through their example, and in writing.

So, as Jesus did, they preached the Gospel; they proclaimed the Good News of God's love for us in Jesus Christ. Also like Jesus, what they preached was accompanied by various deeds: administering baptisms, hearing confessions, celebrating the Eucharist, and performing miracles, such as healing the sick and raising the dead. Those deeds also included (for nearly all of the Apostles) martyrdom (CCC 2473); the Apostles bore witness to the truth of who Jesus was through their willingness to sacrifice their lives for that truth. Finally, in order to ensure that what they had received was handed down faithfully to future generations, the Apostles fulfilled Jesus' commission by writing it down, "under the inspiration of the . . . Holy Spirit."[1] These are the writings that make up the New Testament.

It's important to note that the portion of the Apostolic preaching that was written down didn't exhaust the content of the Gospel, nor did it render their preaching obsolete. Rather, the written word complimented the preached Gospel, allowing the Gospel to be transmitted faithfully as the first generation passed and the Church spread further and further.

Writing down what they preached wasn't the only way the Apostles ensured that their work would continue after they were gone. They also appointed successors, anointing and laying hands on men who would serve the Body of Christ as they themselves did: through teaching, preaching, administering the sacraments, and ensuring that the needs of the Church's most vulnerable members—the poor, the sick, widows, orphans, and the elderly—were met. The Apostles' successors, in turn, had the power to ordain successors of their own, so that the Gospel could be proclaimed in word and deed to every new generation. This process of apostolic succession was explained by the early Church Father St. Irenaeus, who tells us that the Apostles handed over to their successors the authority to teach in their place (see CCC 77).

The Unity of Scripture and Tradition

The Latin word meaning "to hand over" is *tradere*, from which we get

---

[1] Second Vatican Council, Dogmatic Constitution on Divine Revelation *Dei Verbum* (November 18, 1965), §7 (hereafter cited in text as DV).

"tradition." Thus, the Catechism tells us, "This living transmission, accomplished in the Holy Spirit, is called Tradition, since it is distinct from Sacred Scripture, though closely connected to it" (CCC 78). In other words, Sacred Tradition encompasses the handing on, in time, of all the Apostles had received from Jesus' teaching and example, as well as all the knowledge they had received from the Holy Spirit. In short, it is the entirety of the Church's doctrine, life, and worship passed down from bishop to bishop and from age to age.

Both Sacred Scripture and Sacred Tradition share a common source: God himself. The Catechism elaborates:

> Sacred Tradition and Sacred Scripture, then, are bound closely together and communicate one with the other. For both of them, flowing out from the same divine well-spring, come together in some fashion to form one thing, and move towards the same goal [DV 9]. (CCC 80)

Nevertheless, while their source may be the same, their mode of transmission is not. Sacred Scripture "is the speech of God as it is put down in writing under the breath of the Holy Spirit [DV 9]" (CCC 81). Sacred Tradition, on the other hand, is handed down to us by the Church, with the assistance of the Holy Spirit (CCC 81).

Although some people believe that Sacred Scripture and Sacred Tradition are at odds with each other, or that Sacred Scripture is more important than Sacred Tradition, this is not the case. First, because Scripture and Tradition share the same source, they can't be opposed to each other. Truth never contradicts itself. Second, and more fundamentally, Sacred Scripture is part of Sacred Tradition; it's the part that was written down. Sacred Tradition existed before any of the Gospels or Epistles were written; during the first years of the early Church, the Apostles proclaimed the Gospel solely through words and deeds. Moreover, Sacred Tradition assures us of Scripture's authenticity—that the books of the Holy Bible are truly inspired by God.

Scripture, in turn, attests to the importance of Sacred Tradition. "Follow the pattern of the sound words which you have heard from me,"

St. Paul writes; ". . . guard the truth that has been entrusted to you by the Holy Spirit who dwells within us" (2 Tim 1:13–14). He then goes on to advise, "what you have heard from me before many witnesses entrust to faithful men who will be able to teach others also" (2 Tim 2:2).

The Magisterium

Together, "Sacred Tradition and sacred Scripture make up a single sacred deposit of the Word of God, which is entrusted to the Church" (DV 10). The task of interpreting this sacred deposit belongs to the living teaching office of the Church, which is known as the Magisterium (from the Latin word *magister*, meaning teacher).

The Magisterium is "living" in that the Holy Spirit operates through the pope and the bishops in communion with him. While the Holy Spirit doesn't ensure that the pope and the bishops are holy men or that they always do the right thing, the Holy Spirit does prevent the Magisterium from formally teaching error in matters of faith and morals. As such, the Magisterium is not above the Word of God, nor is it a source of Revelation. Rather, it serves the Word of God by teaching it, guarding it, interpreting it, and explaining it to each new generation and always with the help of the Holy Spirit (DV 10).

The Holy Spirit is the common thread that keeps Scripture, Tradition, and the Magisterium working together. The Holy Spirit is the inspirator of Sacred Scripture, the animator of Sacred Tradition, and the guarantor of the Magisterium. That is, he inspired the human authors of Sacred Scripture to write down "whatever he wanted written, and no more" (DV 11). He also guides the Church as she carries on the work of the Apostles, making her worship and sacraments effective means of transmitting grace. Finally, the Holy Spirit guarantees that, in matters of faith and morals, the Magisterium will not formally teach something that is false. In sum, the Holy Spirit ensures that Sacred Scripture, Sacred Tradition, and the Magisterium transmit divine Revelation down through the ages so that even today, two millennia after Jesus came, we can know God's plan and participate in it.

SELECTED READING:

Second Vatican Council, Dogmatic Constitution on Divine Revelation *Dei Verbum* (November 18, 1965), nos. 7–10

God graciously arranged that the things he had once revealed for the salvation of all peoples should remain in their entirety, throughout the ages, and be transmitted to all generations. Therefore, Christ the Lord, in whom the entire Revelation of the most high God is summed up (cf. 2 Cor. 1:20; 3:16–4, 6) commanded the apostles to preach the Gospel, which had been promised beforehand by the prophets, and which he fulfilled in his own person and promulgated with his own lips. In preaching the Gospel they were to communicate the gifts of God to all men. This Gospel was to be the source of all saving truth and moral discipline. This was faithfully done: it was done by the apostles who handed on, by the spoken word of their preaching, by the example they gave, by the institutions they established, what they themselves had received—whether from the lips of Christ, from his way of life and his works, or whether they had learned it at the prompting of the Holy Spirit; it was done by those apostles and other men associated with the apostles who, under the inspiration of the same Holy Spirit, committed the message of salvation to writing.

In order that the full and living Gospel might always be preserved in the Church the apostles left bishops as their successors. They gave them "their own position of teaching authority." This sacred Tradition, then, and the sacred Scripture of both Testaments, are like a mirror, in which the Church, during its pilgrim journey here on earth, contemplates God, from whom she receives everything, until such time as she is brought to see him face to face as he really is (cf. 1 Jn. 3:2).

Thus, the apostolic preaching, which is expressed in a special way in the inspired books, was to be preserved in a continuous line of succession until the end of time. Hence the apostles, in handing on what they themselves had received, warn the faithful to maintain the traditions which they had learned either by word of mouth or by letter (cf. 2 Th. 2:15); and they warn them to fight hard for the faith that had been handed on to them once and for all (cf. Jude 3). What was handed on by the apostles comprises everything that serves to make the People of God live their lives in holiness and increase their faith. In this way the Church, in her doctrine, life and worship, perpetuates and transmits to every generation all that she herself is, all that she believes.

The Tradition that comes from the apostles makes progress in the Church, with the help of the Holy Spirit. There is a growth in insight into the realities and words that are being passed on. This comes about in various ways. It comes through the contemplation and study of believers who ponder these things in their hearts (cf. Lk. 2:19 and 51). It comes from the intimate sense of spiritual realities which they experience. And it comes from the preaching of those who have received, along with their right of succession in the episcopate, the sure charism of truth. Thus, as the centuries go by, the Church is always advancing towards the plenitude of divine truth, until eventually the words of God are fulfilled in her.

The sayings of the Holy Fathers are a witness to the life-giving presence of this Tradition, showing how its riches are poured out in the practice and life of the Church, in her belief and her prayer. By means of the same Tradition the full canon of the sacred books is known to the Church and the holy Scriptures themselves are more thoroughly understood and constantly actualized in the Church. Thus God, who spoke in the past, continues to converse with the spouse of his beloved Son. And the Holy Spirit, through whom the living voice of the Gospel rings out in the Church—and through her in the world—leads believers to the full truth, and makes the Word of Christ dwell in them in all its richness (cf. Col. 3:16).

Sacred Tradition and sacred Scripture, then, are bound closely together, and communicate one with the other. For both of them, flowing out from the same divine well-spring, come together in some fashion to form one thing, and move towards the same goal. Sacred Scripture is the speech of God as it is put down in writing under the breath of the Holy Spirit. And Tradition transmits in its entirety the

Word of God which has been entrusted to the apostles by Christ the Lord and the Holy Spirit. It transmits it to the successors of the apostles so that, enlightened by the Spirit of truth, they may faithfully preserve, expound and spread it abroad by their preaching. Thus it comes about that the Church does not draw her certainty about all revealed truths from the holy Scriptures alone. Hence, both Scripture and Tradition must be accepted and honored with equal feelings of devotion and reverence.

Sacred Tradition and sacred Scripture make up a single sacred deposit of the Word of God, which is entrusted to the Church. By adhering to it the entire holy people, united to its pastors, remains always faithful to the teaching of the apostles, to the brotherhood, to the breaking of bread and the prayers (cf. Acts 2:42 Greek). So, in maintaining, practicing and professing the faith that has been handed on there should be a remarkable harmony between the bishops and the faithful.

But the task of giving an authentic interpretation of the Word of God, whether in its written form or in the form of Tradition, has been entrusted to the living teaching office of the Church alone. Its authority in this matter is exercised in the name of Jesus Christ. Yet this Magisterium is not superior to the Word of God, but is its servant. It teaches only what has been handed on to it. At the divine command and with the help of the Holy Spirit, it listens to this devotedly, guards it with dedication and expounds it faithfully. All that it proposes for belief as being divinely revealed is drawn from this single deposit of faith.

It is clear, therefore, that, in the supremely wise arrangement of God, sacred Tradition, sacred Scripture and the Magisterium of the Church are so connected and associated that one of them cannot stand without the others. Working together, each in its own way under the action of the one Holy Spirit, they all contribute effectively to the salvation of souls.

QUESTIONS FOR REVIEW

1. What was the Great Commission?
2. In what three ways did the Apostles proclaim the Good News?
3. What is Sacred Tradition and how is Sacred Scripture related to it?
4. What is the Magisterium and what does it do?
5. What is the relationship of the Holy Spirit to Sacred Scripture, Sacred Tradition, and the Magisterium?

QUESTIONS FOR DISCUSSION

1. How, through your actions and words, can you fulfill the Great Commission Jesus gave to his followers?
2. Why do our actions matter when proclaiming the Gospel? Why are words not enough?
3. Describe someone you know who is a good witness to the Gospel. What makes their witness effective?

Chapter 3

SACRED SCRIPTURE

We know that divine Revelation is God's revelation of himself to us. We also know that this Revelation comes to us from two sources: Sacred Scripture and Sacred Tradition, both of which are guarded and interpreted by the teaching office of the Church, the Magisterium. What exactly is Sacred Scripture, though? Who is its author? And how is it structured and interpreted?

These are the practical questions about Sacred Scripture that we still need to address before diving into the study of Scripture itself. Let's start by looking at the authorship of Sacred Scripture.

The Authors of Sacred Scripture

Each book of the Bible has, in effect, two authors: a divine author and a human author. God is Scripture's primary author. He didn't just help St. Matthew write his Gospel or give St. Paul editorial advice on his Epistles. He did indeed write the Scriptures. Both the "the books of the Old and the New Testaments, whole and entire," states *Dei Verbum* 11, ". . . have God as their author." St. Paul likewise describes this process of inspiration as *theopneustos*, literally "God-breathed" (2 Tim 3:16).

At the same time, the human authors are still true authors. *Dei Verbum* 11 continues:

> To compose the sacred books, God chose certain men who, all
> the while he employed them in this task, made full use of their
> powers and faculties so that, though he acted in them and by
> them, it was as true authors that they consigned to writing what-
> ever he wanted written, and no more.

It's important to understand that the Bible's human authors weren't like court stenographers. They didn't take down dictation from the Holy Spirit. Instead, as *Dei Verbum* states above, each author brought "their powers and faculties"—their gifts, talents, experiences, and voice—to the text. At the same time, the human authors didn't write down what God wanted them to say and then add in a few thoughts of their own for good measure. They wrote "whatever he wanted written, and no more." Every book and every line in the Bible has a human author and a divine author. And every book and every line reflects everything that both authors wanted to include in the text.

In a certain way, this dual authorship of Scripture—being both fully the work of God and fully the work of man—echoes Jesus himself, the Word made flesh, who is both fully God and fully man. *Dei Verbum* reflects on this connection, noting:

> Indeed the words of God, expressed in the words of men, are in
> every way like human language, just as the Word of the eternal
> Father, when he took on himself the flesh of human weakness,
> became like men. (DV 13)

So, in a sense, as the Word of God (the Second Person of the Trinity) took the form of man in order to identify with us, so too does the Word of God take the form of human words so that we can understand what would otherwise be impossible for our limited nature. This is yet another example of divine "condescension," of a God who "comes down" to our level out of love for us.

God's authorship of Scripture points to another important aspect of the Bible: its inerrancy. This means that what it teaches is guaranteed to be free from all error. This conclusion follows from our understanding of the very nature of God. God, after all, is all good, the fount of all holiness, and the source of truth. Obviously, the source of all truth can't teach something that is wrong; that would be a metaphysical contradiction! The Fathers of Vatican II write:

> Since, therefore, all that the inspired authors, or sacred writers, affirm should be regarded as affirmed by the Holy Spirit, we must acknowledge that the books of Scripture, firmly, faithfully and without error, teach that truth which God, for the sake of our salvation, wished to see confided to the sacred Scriptures. (DV 11)

On the other hand, the Church's teaching about scriptural inerrancy doesn't mean that every statement in the Bible is literally true. We're meant to read some passages as poetry or metaphors. For example, when God calls himself a shepherd, he doesn't intend for us to believe he spends his days in the fields tending sheep. We're supposed to read that as a metaphor about God's love and care for us.

Likewise, the teaching about inerrancy recognizes that the Bible sometimes seems to assert things that seem contradictory to what we know to be true. In these instances, however, it's more a question of interpretation. If there seems to be a contradiction in the text, it may be that we are interpreting it wrong, or have translated it wrong, or simply don't know enough to make a well-formed judgment.

The great Church Father St. Augustine encountered these kinds of contradictions many times in his study of the Scriptures. He explained how he handled them, writing:

> And if in these writings [Scripture] I am perplexed by anything which appears to me opposed to truth, I do not hesitate to suppose that either the manuscript is faulty, or the translator has not caught the meaning of what was said, or I myself have failed to understand it.[1]

---

[1] Augustine, Letter 82.1.3 from Augustine to Jerome (AD 405), http://www.newadvent.org/fathers/1102082.htm.

Ultimately, we need to keep in mind that "the Christian faith is not a 'religion of the book.' Christianity is the religion of the 'Word' of God, a word which is 'not a written and mute word, but the Word which is incarnate and living' [St. Bernard, S. missus est hom. 4,11:PL 183,86]" (CCC 108). It is the Word spoken by God, revealed through Salvation History, and incarnated in time, who is the source of the Bible and Tradition. It is the single Word from the one divine "utterance that resounds in the mouths of all the sacred writers [St. Bernard, S. missus est hom. 4,11:PL 183,86]" who wrote what God intended them to write (CCC 102). Through the Scriptures, it is the Father who "comes lovingly to meet his children, and talks with them" (DV 21). It is in him we trust. It is in him that we put our faith. And it is to him we look to help us interpret the Scriptures.

The Structure of Sacred Scripture

One of the most important things to understand about the Holy Bible is that it is not one book. The actual word "Bible" comes from the Latin biblia, which means books or scrolls, and that's what the Bible is: a collection of many books (and many different types of books), written over the course of more than one thousand years. Some of those books are histories; others are letters, songs, prophecies, wisdom literature, and more. Each book has to be interpreted both on its own terms (as a work of history, prophecy, wisdom literature, etc.), and in the context of the whole Bible.

The books of the Bible themselves are divided into two parts. The first part is the Old Testament, which contains the Jewish Scriptures and is focused on God's work with humanity in general and the Jewish people in particular, from the creation of the world until a couple centuries before the birth of Jesus Christ. The second part is the New Testament, which focuses on the life and ministry of Jesus Christ, as well as the early Church. It contains the Gospels, the Acts of the Apostles, the Epistles, and the Book of Revelation.

The Old Testament canon of Scripture delineated by the Church Fathers and defined at the Council of Trent includes the following forty-six books, which are also listed in paragraph 120 of the Catechism: Genesis, Exodus, Leviticus, Numbers, Deuteronomy, Joshua, Judges, Ruth, 1 and 2 Samuel, 1 and 2 Kings, 1 and 2 Chronicles, Ezra and Nehemiah, Tobit, Judith, Esther, 1 and 2 Maccabees, Job, Psalms, Proverbs, Ecclesiastes, the Song of Songs, the Wisdom of Solomon, Sirach (Ecclesiasticus), Isaiah, Jeremiah, Lamentations, Baruch, Ezekiel, Daniel, Hosea, Joel, Amos, Obadiah, Jonah, Micah, Nahum, Habakkuk, Zephaniah, Haggai, Zachariah, and Malachi.

Old Testament Canon

Pentateuch	Historical Books	Wisdom Books	Prophetic Books	
Genesis	1 & 2 Samuel	Job	Major Prophets:	Minor Prophets:
Exodus	1 & 2 Kings	Psalms	Isaiah	Hosea
Leviticus	1 & 2 Chronicles	Proverbs	Jeremiah	Joel
Numbers	Ezra	Ecclesiastes	Lamentations*	Amos
Deuteronomy	Nehemiah	Song of	Baruch*†	Obadiah
	Tobit†	Songs	Ezekiel	Jonah
	Judith†	Wisdom†	Daniel	Micah
	Esther	Sirach†		Nahum
	1 & 2 Maccabees†			Habakkuk
				Zephaniah
				Haggai
				Zechariah
				Malachi

*Included after Jeremiah; †Deuterocanonical Book

The New Testament canon includes twenty-seven books, which are listed in the Catechism at paragraph 120, as well: the Gospels of Matthew, Mark, Luke, and John; the Acts of the Apostles; the Letters of St. Paul to the Romans, 1 and 2 Corinthians, Galatians, Ephesians, Philippians,

Colossians, 1 and 2 Thessalonians, 1 and 2 Timothy, Titus, Philemon, the Letter to the Hebrews, the Letters of James, 1 and 2 Peter, 1–3 John, Jude, and Revelation (the Apocalypse).

Like the books of the Old Testament, the books of the New Testament are also different "types" of books: the Gospels, the Pauline Epistles, and the "Catholic Letters" (letters written by Apostles other than Paul), along with the Acts of the Apostles and the Book of Revelation.

New Testament Canon

Gospels	Pauline Epistles	Catholic Letters
Matthew	Romans	James
Mark	1 & 2 Corinthians	1 & 2 Peter
Luke	Galatians	1, 2, & 3 John
John	Ephesians	Jude
	Philippians	
	Colossians	
	1 & 2 Thessalonians	
	1 & 2 Timothy†	
	Titus†	
	Philemon †	
	Hebrews**	

Acts of the Apostles*	Revelation*

*These are each in a category of their own

**The authorship of this letter, although not its divine inspiration, is disputed

†These are also known as the Pastoral Letters

The YOUCAT, reflecting upon the differences between these books, explains:

The four Gospels according to Matthew, Mark, Luke, and John are the centerpiece of Sacred Scripture and the most precious treasure of the Church. In them the Son of God shows himself as he is and encounters us. In the Acts of the Apostles we learn about the beginnings of the Church and the working of the Holy Spirit. In the letters written by the apostles, all facets of human life are set in the light of Christ. In the Book of Revelation we foresee the end of the ages.[2]

The Unity of the Old and New Testaments

Like Sacred Scripture and Sacred Tradition, the Old and New Testaments work together to give us a complete picture of Salvation History. Both are essential to understanding how God has worked in time to redeem us and make us holy (CCC 121–123). Each testament helps us understand the other. Each sheds light on the other. They are, the Church teaches, mutually interpreting, with the meaning of the New Testament concealed in the Old and the meaning of the Old Testament revealed and fulfilled in the New. The Church often refers to this way of reading Scripture as "typology."

In his book *Our Father's Plan*, Dr. Scott Hahn explains:

To understand typology, we need to remember that God wrote the world like men write books. He fashioned material objects and events to help us grasp immaterial realities. He created people and things that pointed to spiritual truths. This doesn't mean the people weren't real or the events didn't happen. They were, and they did. But God, as the author of all things, directed human lives and events to point beyond themselves. The authors of the New Testament looked at the people of salvation history, and they saw this. They saw what Saint Paul described

---

[2] Catholic Church, YOUCAT: Youth Catechism of the Catholic Church (San Francisco: Ignatius Press, 2010), 18.

as "types"—a real person, place, or event, which foreshadowed a greater event in the New Testament.[3]

St. Paul introduced this way of reading Scripture in Romans 5:14, when he described Adam as a "type" of Christ. Later, Paul described the Israelites' tabernacle and rituals as types of heavenly realities (Heb 8:5). St. Peter did the same, writing that God's work saving Noah and his family from the flood prefigured Baptism (1 Pet 3:21). The Greek word Peter used for "prefigured" translates as "typify," or literally, "make a type."

Again, typology shows us how the Old Testament explains and illuminates the New Testament, with details from the Old Testament taking on a new importance and significance when read in light of the New Testament. Things like water, fire, doves, gardens, and lambs retain their meaning in the context of the Old Testament, but they also become prefigurements of saving realities: Baptism, the Holy Spirit, Christ on the cross. Likewise, historical biblical figures such as Adam, Isaac, Moses, and David retain their significance in the history of Israel, but they also take on new meaning in the light of Jesus Christ, helping us understand what he accomplished through his life, death, and Resurrection.

From the very first, the Church has used this way of reading the Scriptures to understand God's saving plan. The Catechism of the Catholic Church explains:

Christians therefore read the Old Testament in the light of Christ crucified and risen . . . [and] the New Testament has to be read in the light of the Old. Early Christian catechesis made constant use of the Old Testament [Cf. *1 Cor* 5:6–8; 1-:1–11]. As an old saying put it, the New Testament lies hidden in the Old and the Old Testament is unveiled in the New [Cf. St. Augustine, *Quaest. in Hept.* 2,73:PL 34,623; Cf. *DV* 16]. (129)

---

[3]   Scott Hahn, *The Mystery of Faith* (forthcoming).

The Canon of Sacred Scripture

All of this raises the question: How do we know which books are divinely inspired? How do we know that these books, and only these books, are truly *Sacred* Scripture?

During the first several centuries after Jesus' death and Resurrection, there was no one definitive list of which books were or weren't Sacred Scripture. Different Jewish communities recognized different lists of Jewish Scripture as inspired by God, while different Gospels and writings circulated among Christian communities. By and large, however, despite these differences, there still existed a widespread consensus among Christians about which books were and were not considered divinely inspired.

This consensus was formalized by the Magisterium repeatedly, beginning with the Council of Rome in 382. There, as well as at the Council of Hippo in 393, the Third Council of Carthage in 397, and the Fourth Council of Carthage in 418, the Church's bishops made clear which books attributed to the prophets and Apostles were divinely inspired. Their primary criteria for making that determination was the liturgy. The books affirmed as inspired were those that had been read in the Church's liturgy since the very beginning. Likewise, the primary reason the Church initially felt compelled to declare an official canon of Scripture was for the liturgy: the Christian communities growing and spreading across the Roman Empire needed to know which books they could read in the Mass. The Church's various councils in the fourth and fifth centuries settled that question for them.

Over one thousand years later, after the Protestant "reformers" sought to remove certain books from the Bible—ironically because they believed them to contain "unbiblical" teachings—the Magisterium once more addressed the question. On April 8, 1546, in the fourth session of the Council of Trent, the Church reiterated which books did and did not belong to the official list of scriptural books—also known as the "canon." Echoing the early Church Fathers, the Fathers of Trent officially declared the same forty-six books of the Old Testament and twenty-seven books of the New Testament divinely inspired and therefore canonical.

Remember, the Magisterium is able to make affirmations like this because of the Holy Spirit. He guarantees the Magisterium's authority, ensuring that the Church's bishops in union with the pope infallibly interpret, guard, and preserve the deposit of faith that comes to us in Scripture and Tradition.

As for the canon itself, the Church's Old Testament canon is primarily based on the Septuagint, which was the version of the Jewish Scriptures in common use among both the Hellenist (Greek-speaking) Jews, in places such as Rome and Alexandria, and the early Christians. The Septuagint included translations of the biblical books that had been written in Hebrew (with the exception of a few chapters in Aramaic) plus newer books that had been written in Greek. These newer books were not included in the Masoretic version of the Scriptures, used by non-Hellenist Jews and later adopted by Protestants. For this reason, the Books of Tobit, Judith, Sirach, Wisdom, Baruch, and 1 and 2 Maccabees, as well as additional parts of Esther and Daniel, are considered canonical by Catholics, as well as the Orthodox and other Eastern Christians, but not by Protestants and modern-day Jews. Catholics often refer to the seven books as "deuterocanonical," which literally means "second canon," while Protestants refer to them as "apocryphal" or "the apocrypha."

Unlike the Old Testament, there is no disagreement between Catholics and Protestants about which books belong in the New Testament. Nevertheless, because "the Gospels are at the heart of all the Scriptures" (CCC 125), not only in meaning and importance but also in their location in the Bible, it's helpful to understand how they were formed.

The first stage in their formation is the *life and teaching of Jesus*. This includes all that he taught up until he ascended into heaven. The second stage is the *oral tradition*, which is what the Apostles preached after the Ascension. Filled with the Holy Spirit, they were able to experience a greater understanding of what Jesus said and did, and they were empowered to communicate that message (the Good News) to people through their preaching (CCC 126). The third stage is the *written Gospels*, which, according to *Dei Verbum*, took place in the following manner:

The sacred authors, in writing the four Gospels, selected certain of the many elements which had been handed on, either orally or already in written form, others they synthesized or explained with an eye to the situation of the churches, the while sustaining the form of preaching, but always in such a fashion that they have told us the honest truth about Jesus. (DV 19)

SELECTED READING:
Second Vatican Council, *Dei Verbum*, nos. 11–13

The divinely revealed realities, which are contained and presented in the text of sacred Scripture, have been written down under the inspiration of the Holy Spirit. For Holy Mother Church relying on the faith of the apostolic age, accepts as sacred and canonical the books of the Old and the New Testaments, whole and entire, with all their parts, on the grounds that, written under the inspiration of the Holy Spirit (cf. Jn. 20:31; 2 Tim. 3:16; 2 Pet. 1:19–21; 3:15–16), they have God as their author, and have been handed on as such to the Church herself. To compose the sacred books, God chose certain men who, all the while he employed them in this task, made full use of their powers and faculties so that, though he acted in them and by them, it was as true authors that they consigned to writing whatever he wanted written, and no more.

Since, therefore, all that the inspired authors, or sacred writers, affirm should be regarded as affirmed by the Holy Spirit, we must acknowledge that the books of Scripture, firmly, faithfully and without error, teach that truth which God, for the sake of our salvation, wished to see confided to the sacred Scriptures. Thus "all Scripture is inspired by God, and profitable for teaching, for reproof, for correction and for training in righteousness, so that the man of God may be complete, equipped for every good work" (2 Tim. 3:16–17, Gk. text).

Seeing that, in sacred Scripture, God speaks through men in human fashion, it follows that the interpreter of sacred Scriptures, if he is to ascertain what God has wished to communicate to us, should carefully search out the meaning which the sacred writers really had in mind, that meaning which God had thought well to manifest through the medium of their words.

In determining the intention of the sacred writers, attention must be paid, inter alia, to "literary forms for the fact is that truth is differently presented and expressed in the various types of histori- cal writing, in prophetical and poetical texts," and in other forms of literary expression. Hence the exegete must look for that meaning which the sacred writer, in a determined situation and given the cir- cumstances of his time and culture, intended to express and did in fact express, through the medium of a contemporary literary form. Rightly to understand what the sacred author wanted to affirm in his work, due attention must be paid both to the customary and charac- teristic patterns of perception, speech and narrative which prevailed at the age of the sacred writer, and to the conventions which the people of his time followed in their dealings with one another.

But since sacred Scripture must be read and interpreted with its divine authorship in mind no less attention must be devoted to the content and unity of the whole of Scripture, taking into account the Tradition of the entire Church and the analogy of faith, if we are to derive their true meaning from the sacred texts. It is the task of exe- getes to work, according to these rules, towards a better understand- ing and explanation of the meaning of sacred Scripture in order that their research may help the Church to form a firmer judgment. For, of course, all that has been said about the manner of interpreting Scripture is ultimately subject to the judgment of the Church which exercises the divinely conferred commission and ministry of watch- ing over and interpreting the Word of God.

Hence, in sacred Scripture, without prejudice to God's truth and holiness, the marvellous "condescension" of eternal wisdom is plain to be seen "that we may come to know the ineffable loving-kindness of God and see for ourselves how far he has gone in adapting his lan- guage with thoughtful concern for our nature." Indeed the words of God, expressed in the words of men, are in every way like human lan- guage, just as the Word of the eternal Father, when he took on himself the flesh of human weakness, became like men.

QUESTIONS FOR REVIEW

1. Who is the primary author of Sacred Scripture?
2. What are the two "parts" of Sacred Scripture?
3. What is typology? Define and give one example.
4. When determining which books belonged in the Bible, what was the primary criteria?
5. What were the three stages in the formation of the Gospels?

QUESTIONS FOR DISCUSSION

1. What are some of the ways you communicate to others who you are, what you feel, and what you desire?
2. How does it feel when people don't hear or understand what you are communicating?
3. Given all that God did to communicate the truth about himself to us, what should our response to him be?

Chapter 4

THE INTERPRETATION OF SACRED SCRIPTURE

Biblical Criticism

It is one thing to read the Scriptures. It is another thing to interpret and understand what their true meaning is supposed to be. Accordingly, whenever we approach the Holy Bible, we must examine and "be attentive to what the human authors truly wanted to affirm, and to what God wanted to reveal to us by their words" (CCC 109). This means that we must take into consideration the context of the passage, the literary forms, and the writers' intentions (CCC 110).

To discover the human author's meaning, we can take advantage of a variety of methods of biblical and literary analysis. Among these are different schools and methods of biblical criticism. The word "criticism" can be misleading, because it can sound like we're criticizing or critiquing the text. Really, though, it just means that we're studying it and trying to come to a better understanding of the text and what it says. This type of studying most often takes one of two forms: historical criticism and literary criticism.

Historical criticism looks at the historical context of a book or passage, examining what the cultural, political, and sociological events and trends of the time when the passage was written tell us about the passage. Literary criticism looks at the composition of the text. It uses language, genres, figures of speech, allusions, and more to shed light on the meaning of biblical passages. We also can combine the two methods and use them at the same time. For example, we could examine common types of literature in different historical eras or specific words used in a certain time period.

These methods, when used well, help shed light on the human meaning of certain passages and even books of Scripture. However, as the *Catholic Bible Dictionary* explains:

> Though essential to the task, the critical methods are by no means fully sufficient to discover the full meaning of Scripture. Interpretation must ultimately go beyond the critical disciplines to consider the divine realities of the Word, to listen for the voice of God speaking through its various modes of human speech. Failure to do this often leads to a biblical exegesis that is sterile and lifeless, having nothing to inspire faith or to encourage a deeper commitment to the Lord. It must always be remembered that the Bible, though truly human, is not merely human. The text of Scripture is indeed a rich source of human information, but its ultimate goal is human salvation.[1]

Basically, we need to remember that the Bible is not merely a book. It is truly Sacred Scripture, which means that if we truly want to grow in our understanding of it, studying it from an academic perspective isn't enough. We also must, in a sense, pray our way through the Bible, contemplating it, meditating upon it, and being open to the guidance of the Holy Spirit. After all, the Holy Spirit is the one who inspired Sacred Scripture, so he is our best help in understanding it.

---

[1] Scott Hahn, ed., "Biblical Criticism," in *Catholic Bible Dictionary* (New York: Double-day, 2009), 113.

Principles of Interpretation

At the Second Vatican Council, the bishops of the world sought to address many of the problems that have arisen in recent times when scholars have attempted to "interpret" the Bible apart from the unity of Scripture and the living Tradition of the Church. To help Catholic scholars going forward, they laid out a number of principles for biblical interpretation. The three most important principles they gave us are:

1. *"Be especially attentive 'to the content and unity of the whole Scripture.'"* (CCC 112)

This means we must read the biblical text in context—not just in the context of the chapter or the book in which we find it, but also in the context of the whole of the Bible and the whole of God's plan. We can't separate the part from the whole. Instead, we need to recognize that every line in the Bible has something to tell us about the whole of Salvation History, and that the whole of Salvation History has something to tell us about every line in the Bible.

2. *"Read the Scripture 'within the living Tradition of the whole Church.'"* (CCC 113)

As we discussed already, Sacred Scripture is the written expression of God's revelation. Before a single Gospel or Epistle was penned, the words those books contained were proclaimed by the Apostles in word and deed. They are, in a sense, a memorial of what the Apostles received from Jesus and the Holy Spirit and of what they, in turn, handed on to their successors. They belong to the Church and were proclaimed since the first days of the Church in her liturgy. In that same liturgy, the Old Testament was read and proclaimed alongside the New, with each Testament shedding light on the other, helping make sense of the whole of Salvation History. As such, guided by the Spirit, the Church interprets Scripture within the living Tradition. Biblical scholars must do likewise.

3. *"Be attentive to the analogy of faith [Cf. Rom 12:6.]."* (CCC 114)

In short, remember that the doctrines of the faith cannot contradict each other. There is always an inner consistency, and scholars must look for that. In doing so, they should keep in mind that all the doctrines of the faith are also interconnected. Each illuminates the other. Accordingly, when one doctrine seems dark or impenetrable, scholars should turn to the other doctrines that can shed light on it.

In the end, the Church is the proper setting for the interpretation of Scripture. It is the Church who wrote the New Testament and who then collected, approved, and handed on the canon of Scriptures. The Bible is the Church's book. It was written from her heart (CCC 113). As such, Pope Benedict XVI explains:

> The Holy Spirit, who gives life to the Church, enables us to interpret the Scriptures authoritatively. The Bible is the Church's book, and its essential place in the Church's life gives rise to its genuine interpretation.[2]

The Senses of Sacred Scripture

Another key to reading and interpreting the Bible rightly is to understand the different "senses of Scripture." There are, broadly speaking, two different "senses": the literal sense and the spiritual sense.

The first sense is the literal sense. This means what the words on the page are literally saying, or as the Catechism describes it: "the meaning conveyed by the words of Scripture and discovered by exegesis, following the rules of sound interpretation" (CCC 116). Sometimes, the literal sense of a passage is plain: "Jesus wept" means just that—Jesus wept. Other times, though, historical context, literary forms, or cultural and linguistic differences make it more challenging to understand a passage's literal meaning. This is where the different forms of criticism described above can prove helpful.

The second sense of Scripture is the spiritual sense. When we look for the spiritual sense of a particular passage in Scripture, we're looking for the meaning that goes beyond the literal words on the page and sheds

---

[2] Pope Benedict XVI, Post-Synodal Apostolic Exhortation on the Word of God in the Life and Mission of the Church *Verbum Domini* (September 30, 2010), 29.

light on spiritual truths. Importantly, the spiritual sense can never contradict the literal sense of Scripture. As St. Thomas Aquinas wrote, "All other senses of Scripture are based on the literal."[3] The spiritual sense can, however, reveal a deeper or complementary meaning to the passage, showing us a depth we didn't first perceive when we read the words.

The spiritual sense of Scripture is actually subdivided into three categories: the allegorical, moral (or tropological), and anagogical (CCC 117). This means that, in addition to the literal meaning, a scriptural passage also can convey a truth about the life or person of Christ (allegorical); a truth about how Christians should live (moral); and a truth about heaven (anagogical).

Recognizing these different spiritual senses helps us more fully understand the words of Sacred Scripture. It also helps us grow closer to Jesus as we read the Bible. As the Church teaches, perceiving the allegorical sense enriches our faith, helping us to know Jesus better; perceiving the moral sense helps us grow in charity, for we learn more about how God wants us to live; and perceiving the anagogical sense helps us to grow in hope, because it reminds us to keep an eternal perspective on things.

Applying the Different Senses of Scripture

How, though, do we distinguish these different senses of Scripture when we're reading the Bible? What does this type of spiritual exegesis—or spiritual interpretation of a scriptural text—look like in practice?

To answer that question, let's look at the story of the binding of Isaac, known as the *Aqedah* (Gen 22:1–19). The literal sense is the story; it's what happens. God orders Abraham to sacrifice his only "beloved" son, Isaac. Abraham obeys. He takes his son into the wilderness, and together they walk up Mount Moriah, with Isaac carrying the wood that Abraham plans to use for the sacrifice. One important insight this literal sense gives us is that Isaac wasn't a small boy. If he was strong enough to carry the wood, he was already an adolescent or young adult, meaning that

---

[3] Thomas Aquinas, *Summa Theologiae* I, q. 1, a. 10, ad I, quoted in CCC 116.

he could have easily overpowered his elderly father and resisted being bound and tied to the wood. But he doesn't do that. Instead, he accepts his father's will and prepares to allow himself to be sacrificed. At the last minute, though, an angel stays Abraham's hand and a ram presents itself to be offered in Isaac's place.

That's the literal meaning of the text. But, when we read the story through the filter of the other spiritual senses, we find further layers of meaning.

First, examining the allegorical sense, we can see that the story points to Jesus, who was the only beloved Son of God. Like Isaac, Jesus willingly carried the wood for his sacrifice—his cross—up the hill where he would be crucified, doing so out of obedience to his Father.

Second, looking at the passage's moral sense reminds us that each of us have crosses to bear in this life. Like Isaac, we are called to accept these crosses out of love and obedience to God, our Father, trusting he will use the graces merited by our sufferings to bring help and salvation to others.

Finally, interpreting the anagogical sense of the *Aqedah* helps us understand that carrying our cross is part of our journey to holiness. Each of us must walk the path of self-sacrifice if we hope to spend an eternity with God in heaven. Like Abraham, we must be willing to trust in God's plan, and like Isaac, we must hold nothing more dear than our Father's will.

This type of literal and spiritual exegesis can help us understand all of Sacred Scripture better. It illuminates God's plan for our salvation, showing us how all Salvation History points to Jesus Christ. It also illuminates our life here, now, on earth, reminding us of the rich guidance we can find in Sacred Scripture for how to live good and loving lives. Lastly, it helps us keep our eye on heaven, reminding us that the joys and sorrows of this life are passing, and helping us see everything from the perspective of heaven.

SELECTED READING

Pope Benedict XVI, Post-Synodal Apostolic Exhortation
on the Word of God in the Life and Mission of the Church
Verbum Domini (September 30, 2010), nos. 35–36

In this regard we should mention the serious risk nowadays of a
dualistic approach[4] to sacred Scripture. To distinguish two levels
of approach to the Bible does not in any way mean to separate or
oppose them, nor simply to juxtapose them. They exist only in
reciprocity. Unfortunately, a sterile separation sometimes creates a
barrier between exegesis and theology, and this "occurs even at the
highest academic levels." Here I would mention the most troubling
consequences, which are to be avoided.

a) First and foremost, if the work of exegesis is restricted to
the first level alone, Scripture ends up being *a text belonging only to
the past*: "One can draw moral consequences from it, one can learn
history, but the Book as such speaks only of the past, and exegesis is
no longer truly theological, but becomes pure historiography, history
of literature." Clearly, such a reductive approach can never make it
possible to comprehend the event of God's revelation through his
word, which is handed down to us in the living Tradition and in
Scripture.

b) The lack of a hermeneutic of faith with regard to Scripture
entails more than a simple absence; in its place there inevitably
enters another hermeneutic, a positivistic and *secularized hermeneutic*[5] ultimately based on the conviction that the Divine does not
intervene in human history. According to this hermeneutic, whenever a divine element seems present, it has to be explained in some
other way, reducing everything to the human element. This leads to
interpretations that deny the historicity of the divine elements.

c) Such a position can only prove harmful to the life of the

---

4   Here Pope Benedict XVI is referring to studying Scripture exclusively as an historical
    document or exclusively as a religious document.
5   Secularized hermeneutic: interpreting the Bible apart from the Church's faith, as
    though it's a merely human document.

Church, casting doubt over fundamental mysteries of Christianity and their historicity—as, for example, the institution of the Eucharist and the resurrection of Christ. A philosophical hermeneutic is thus imposed, one which denies the possibility that the Divine can enter and be present within history. The adoption of this hermeneutic within theological studies inevitably introduces a sharp dichotomy between an exegesis limited solely to the first level and a theology tending towards a spiritualization of the meaning of the Scriptures, one which would fail to respect the historical character of revelation.

All this is also bound to have a negative impact on the spiritual life and on pastoral activity; "as a consequence of the absence of the second methodological level, a profound gulf is opened up between scientific exegesis and *lectio divina*. This can give rise to a lack of clarity in the preparation of homilies." It must also be said that this dichotomy can create confusion and a lack of stability in the intellectual formation of candidates for ecclesial ministries. In a word, "where exegesis is not theology, Scripture cannot be the soul of theology, and conversely, where theology is not essentially the interpretation of the Church's Scripture, such a theology no longer has a foundation." Hence we need to take a more careful look at the indications provided by the Dogmatic Constitution *Dei Verbum* in this regard.

I believe that what Pope John Paul II wrote about this question in his Encyclical *Fides et Ratio* can lead to a fuller understanding of exegesis and its relationship to the whole of theology. He stated that we should not underestimate "the danger inherent in seeking to derive the truth of sacred Scripture from the use of one method alone, ignoring the need for a more comprehensive exegesis which enables the exegete, together with the whole Church, to arrive at the full sense of the texts. Those who devote themselves to the study of sacred Scripture should always remember that the various hermeneutical approaches have their own philosophical underpinnings, which need to be carefully evaluated before they are applied to the sacred texts."

This far-sighted reflection enables us to see how a hermeneutical approach to sacred Scripture inevitably brings into play the proper relationship between faith and reason. Indeed, the secularized hermeneutic of sacred Scripture is the product of reason's attempt structurally to exclude any possibility that God might enter into our lives and speak to us in human words. Here too, we need to urge a *broadening of the scope of reason*. In applying methods of historical analysis, no criteria should be adopted which would rule out in advance God's self-disclosure in human history. The unity of the two levels at work in the interpretation of sacred Scripture presupposes, in a word, *the harmony of faith and reason*. On the one hand, it calls for a faith which, by maintaining a proper relationship with right reason, never degenerates into fideism,[6] which in the case of Scripture would end up in fundamentalism. On the other hand, it calls for a reason which, in its investigation of the historical elements present in the Bible, is marked by openness and does not reject a priori anything beyond its own terms of reference. In any case, the religion of the incarnate *Logos*[7] can hardly fail to appear profoundly reasonable to anyone who sincerely seeks the truth and the ultimate meaning of his or her own life and history.

---

[6] Fideism is blind faith apart from the exercise of reason.

[7] *Logos* means "the Word," which is how Jesus is referred to in the Gospel of John (Jn 1:1). The incarnate *Logos* is God made flesh in Jesus (Jn 1:14).

QUESTIONS FOR REVIEW

1. What is historical criticism?
2. What is literary criticism?
3. What three principles for biblical interpretation did the Second Vatican Council outline?
4. What does the literal sense of Scripture mean?
5. What are the different spiritual senses of Scripture?

QUESTIONS FOR DISCUSSION

1. When reading the Bible, do you think we should treat it just like any other book? Why or why not?
2. When you approach the Bible, what is your attitude? Do you trust it? Are you suspicious? Reverent? Explain why.
3. Have you ever read a book more than once? If so, explain what you learned from the second reading that you didn't take away from the first reading. How could reading the Bible many times benefit us?

Chapter 5

THE ROLE OF SCRIPTURE IN THE LIFE OF THE CHURCH

Sacred Scripture is the Word of God inspired by the Holy Spirit for the sake of our salvation. As such, the words, prayers, teachings, and people of Sacred Scripture are woven into the entire fabric of the Church's life. They are part of everything the Church says and does. Indeed, *Dei Verbum* tells us:

> The Church has always venerated the divine Scriptures as she venerated the Body of the Lord, in so far as she never ceases, particularly in the sacred liturgy, to partake of the bread of life and to offer it to the faithful from the one table of the Word of God and the Body of Christ. (21)

This reverence for Sacred Scripture is evident first and foremost in the Church's liturgy, starting with the Holy Mass. From first to last, the Mass is filled with verses and passages from the Bible. The readings, the psalm, and the Gospel come exclusively from the Scriptures. So too do the prayers and antiphons: the words of the Kyrie ("Lord have mercy") echo the cries of the Canaanite woman in Matthew 15:22. The Gloria features the joyful words that the angels cried out at Jesus' birth (Luke 2:14). The Sanctus ("Holy, Holy, Holy)" is the song of the angels in heaven in Revelation 4:8. The words we pray before communion, "Lord I am not worthy that you should enter under my roof," are the words spoken to Jesus by the Centurion in Matthew 8:8. And the words of the consecration ("This is my body . . . This is my blood") are those spoken by Jesus in the Upper Room on the night before he died when he first instituted the Sacrament of the Eucharist (Matt 26:26–28; Mark 14:22–24; Luke 22:19–20).

These are just a few of the many uses of Scripture in the Mass. But, even more important, much of what is in the Bible is actually enacted and *made present* through the Mass. In the Mass, we worship Jesus with the angels, as in the Book of Revelation. And in the Mass, Jesus does come again to us, giving himself to us under the appearance of bread and wine.

The reverse can also be said. Not only are the Scriptures of the utmost importance to the Mass, but the Mass is also of the utmost importance to the Scriptures, since "liturgy enjoys a unity with Scripture that is indissoluble."[1] In other words, the Scriptures and the liturgy are so interrelated that the Church "duly fosters the study of the Fathers, both Eastern and Western, and of the sacred liturgies" (DV 23) so that we can better understand the Sacred Scriptures. Just as knowledge of the Bible helps us understand what is taking place in the liturgy, knowledge of the liturgy can help us understand the Bible.

In addition to the Mass, the Scriptures are also integral to the Liturgy of the Hours. Also known as the Divine Office, the Liturgy of the Hours is the universal, public prayer of the Church. Priests and religious pray it every day, and the laity are encouraged to pray it as well, whether in whole or part, allowing the biblical readings and meditations to draw us closer to Jesus and sanctify the hours of the day.

Then, of course, there are the traditional prayers of the Church, which draw upon Scripture: the Our Father (Matt 6:9–15; Luke 11:2–4); the Hail Mary (Luke 1:28, 42); and the Angelus. The Rosary not only uses these scriptural prayers, but calls us to pray them while meditating upon twenty different events from the life of Christ.

Last but not least, all the preaching and teaching of the Church is "nourished and ruled by sacred Scripture" (DV 21), with the Church seeing the study of Scripture as "the very soul of sacred theology" (DV 24). Scripture

---

[1] Scott Hahn and Leo Suprenant, Jr., eds., *Scripture and the Mystery of the Mother of God*, Catholic for a Reason (Steubenville, OH: Emmaus Road Publishing, 2004), 272.

is what priests are instructed to preach about in their homilies, and Scripture informs the writing, research, and teaching of all her theologians. This is because the goal of all the Church's teaching—her preaching, homilies, catechesis, and writing—is to bring people into a relationship with Jesus Christ, the Word of God made flesh. An encounter with the written Word of God makes that possible.

Scripture is an integral part of the Church because the Church is missionary, meaning that it must "go out" and spread the Gospel as Jesus instructed (Mark 16:15). Vatican II's Dogmatic Constitution on Divine Revelation ends with this hope for the Church:

> So may it come that, by the reading and study of the sacred books "the Word of God may speed on and triumph" (2 Th. 3:1) and the treasure of Revelation entrusted to the Church may more and more fill the hearts of men. Just as from constant attendance at the eucharistic mystery the life of the Church draws increase, so a new impulse of spiritual life may be expected from increased veneration of the Word of God, which "stands forever" (Is. 40:8; cf. 1 Pet. 1:23–25). (DV 26)

How to Use the Sacred Scriptures

When you want to grow closer to a person, you try to learn about them. If there is something written about the person, you read it. If you can spend time with them, you do. And if you can talk with them and listen to them, you do that as well. In the case of getting to know Jesus, the same holds true.

To get to know Jesus, we can read about his life in the Gospels, spend time prayerfully contemplating his actions, listen to his words, and listen to words others wrote about him. In this way, we follow the advice of St. Ambrose of Milan, who wrote, "we speak to [God] when we pray; we listen to him when we read the divine oracles [Sacred Scripture]" (DV 25; see CCC 2653). Thus, we enter into a true dialogue with God.

With this prayerful communication in mind, here is a list of a few ways to use the Bible:

- Read it on your own in the morning or in the evening before bed. A good place to start is with the Gospels, followed by the Epistles. Another place to start would be with a narrative approach, sticking with the narrative books outlined in the Bible timeline on the next page, which would give you the big picture of Salvation History.

- Read the readings for Mass each day, using the Catholic Lectionary. This will enable you to read the majority of the Bible over a span of three years and unite you each day to the liturgy of the Church. Likewise, taking a look at the readings before Mass can help prepare your heart and mind for whatever God wants you to receive from him in the readings and homily.

- *Lectio Divina* is a practice that dates back to at least the sixth century. It involves reading a passage of Scripture (looking at what the text states), meditating upon it (seeing what the text says to you), praying about what you've read (responding to the Lord), and contemplating what you've read and meditated upon (reflecting even more deeply upon what God is showing you and asking you to do). Pope Benedict XVI wrote about the importance of this in his apostolic exhortation *Verbum Domini*.

- Read Scripture in the presence of the Lord at adoration. This way, in addition to learning about Jesus, you get to spend time with him in the Eucharist, where he is truly present in Body, Blood, Soul, and Divinity.

- Read it with others. This can be done as a family, with friends, or in a Bible study. Reading the Bible with others is a great way to discuss certain passages and learn to apply the Word of God to your life.

- Memorize certain passages or pieces of Scripture. Writing down verses and keeping them in front of us (for example, on a mirror, as a wallpaper on our phone, or in a notebook) keeps the Word of God on our minds and in our hearts, especially in times of temptation or despair, or when we need a reminder of how God wants us to live.

- Pray the Rosary. When praying the mysteries of the Rosary, you are really meditating upon parts of Scripture, reflecting upon the events of Jesus' life in the midst of your own life.

The Twelve Periods of Salvation History

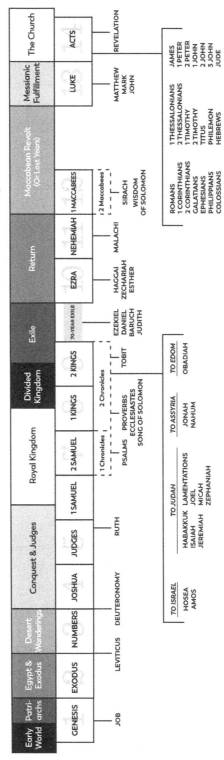

Responding to the Sacred Scriptures

In the Holy Bible, God reveals himself to us. He shares his fatherly heart with us, showing us how he has fathered the human race from age to age, helping us to grow in maturity and wisdom so that we can receive the greatest gift he could possibly give us: himself, in the person of Jesus Christ.

Each of us, individually, is called to receive that gift. We are called to respond to God's invitation to know him and love him in Jesus with faith and love.

To respond with faith means saying yes to God and all he asks of us, readily obeying his commandments and trusting his plan for our salvation. The Catechism calls this the "obedience of faith," noting that "to obey (from the Latin *ob-audire*, to 'hear or listen to') in faith is to submit freely to the word that has been heard, because its truth is guaranteed by God, who is Truth itself" (144). Because the Bible is inspired by God, there can be no higher standard or instruction by which to live. There can be no greater guide for our journey in this life.

Likewise, to respond with love is to follow that guide not simply out of obedience, but out of a genuine desire to grow closer to God. The obedience we give God shouldn't be grudging, but trusting. We should trust that he has our very best interest in mind, that he is doing all he can to give us that very best, even if we don't fully understand how he is doing that. The obedience of faith is, at its most basic level, the obedience of a loving, trusting child who places their hand in the hand of their father and joyfully follows him, knowing he will never lead them astray.

While each of us is called individually to give God this obedience, we don't have to give it alone. In fact, we aren't supposed to give it alone. Rather, God calls us to live and believe in community with others, mutually encouraging each other in this walk of faith. The Catechism explains:

Faith is a personal act—the free response of the human person to the initiative of God who reveals himself. But faith is not an isolated act. No one can believe alone, just as no one can live alone. You have not given yourself faith as you have not given yourself life. . . . Each believer is thus a link in the great chain of believers. I cannot believe without being carried by the faith of others, and by my faith I help support others in the faith. (CCC 166)

Following the example of Mary, who, while carrying Jesus in her womb, rushed off to help her pregnant cousin Elizabeth, each of us is called to carry Christ to others. We are all called to be Christ-bearers, bringing his message of love and salvation to the world. The more we allow God's Word to fill us and form us, the more readily we can answer that call.

In order to carry out that task with greater love and knowledge, however, we need to know the Scriptures. We need to know what God reveals to us through his Word. So, to the Scriptures themselves we now turn.

SELECTED READING
Pope Benedict XVI, *Verbum Domini*, nos. 86–87

The Synod frequently insisted on the need for a prayerful approach to the sacred text as a fundamental element in the spiritual life of every believer, in the various ministries and states in life, with particular reference to *lectio divina*. The word of God is at the basis of all authentic Christian spirituality. The Synod Fathers thus took up the words of the Dogmatic Constitution *Dei Verbum*: "Let the faithful go gladly to the sacred text itself, whether in the sacred liturgy, which is full of the divine words, or in devout reading, or in such suitable exercises and various other helps which, with the approval and guidance of the pastors of the Church, are happily spreading everywhere in our day. Let them remember, however, that prayer should accompany the reading of sacred Scripture." The Council thus sought to reappropriate the great patristic tradition which had always recommended approaching the Scripture in dialogue with God. As Saint Augustine puts it: "Your prayer is the word you speak to God. When you read the Bible, God speaks to you; when you pray, you speak to God." Origen, one of the great masters of this way of reading the Bible, maintains that understanding Scripture demands, even more than study, closeness to Christ and prayer. Origen was convinced, in fact, that the best way to know God is through love, and that there can be no authentic *scientia Christi* [knowledge of Christ] apart from growth in his love. In his *Letter to Gregory*, the great Alexandrian theologian gave this advice: "Devote yourself to the *lectio* of the divine Scriptures; apply yourself to this with perseverance. Do your reading with the intent of believing in and pleasing God. If during the *lectio* you encounter a closed door, knock and it will be opened to you by that guardian of whom Jesus said, 'The gatekeeper will open it for him.' By applying yourself in this way to *lectio divina*, search diligently and with unshakable trust in God for the meaning of the divine Scriptures, which is hidden in great fullness within. You ought not, however, to be satisfied merely with knocking and seeking: to understand the things of God, what is absolutely necessary is *oratio*. For this reason, the Saviour told us not only: 'Seek and you will find,' and 'Knock and it shall be opened to you,' but also added, 'Ask and you shall receive.'"

In this regard, however, one must *avoid the risk of an individualistic approach,* and remember that God's word is given to us precisely to build communion, to unite us in the Truth along our path to God. While it is a word addressed to each of us personally, it is also a word which builds community, which builds the Church. Consequently, *the sacred text must always be approached in the communion of the Church.* In effect, "a communal reading of Scripture is extremely important, because the living subject in the sacred Scriptures is the People of God, it is the Church . . . Scripture does not belong to the past, because its subject, the People of God inspired by God himself, is always the same, and therefore the word is always alive in the living subject. As such, it is important to read and experience sacred Scripture in communion with the Church, that is, with all the great witnesses to this word, beginning with the earliest Fathers up to the saints of our own day, up to the present-day magisterium."

For this reason, *the privileged place* for the prayerful reading of sacred Scripture *is the liturgy*, and particularly *the Eucharist*, in which, as we celebrate the Body and Blood of Christ in the sacrament, the word itself is present and at work in our midst. In some sense the prayerful reading of the Bible, personal and communal, must always be related to the Eucharistic celebration. Just as the adoration of the Eucharist prepares for, accompanies and follows the liturgy of the Eucharist, so too prayerful reading, personal and communal, prepares for, accompanies and deepens what the Church celebrates when she proclaims the word in a liturgical setting. By so closely relating *lectio* and liturgy, we can better grasp the criteria which should guide this practice in the area of pastoral care and in the spiritual life of the People of God.

The documents produced before and during the Synod mentioned a number of methods for a faith-filled and fruitful approach to sacred Scripture. Yet the greatest attention was paid to *lectio divina*, which is truly "capable of opening up to the faithful the treasures of God's word, but also of bringing about an encounter with Christ, the living word of God." I would like here to review the basic steps of this procedure. It opens with the reading (*lectio*) of a text, which leads to a desire to understand its true content: *what does the biblical text say in itself?* Without this, there is always a risk that the text will become a pretext for never moving beyond our own ideas. Next comes meditation (*meditatio*), which asks: *what does the biblical text say to us?* Here, each person, individually but also as a member of the community, must let himself or herself be moved and challenged. Following this comes prayer (*oratio*), which asks the question: *what do we say to the Lord in response to his word?* Prayer, as petition, intercession, thanksgiving and praise, is the primary way by which the word transforms us. Finally, *lectio divina* concludes with contemplation (*contemplatio*), during which we take up, as a gift from God, his own way of seeing and judging reality, and ask ourselves *what conversion of mind, heart and life is the Lord asking of us?* In the *Letter to the Romans*, Saint Paul tells us: "Do not be conformed to this world, but be transformed by the renewal of your mind, that you may prove what is the will of God, what is good and acceptable and perfect"

(12:2). Contemplation aims at creating within us a truly wise and discerning vision of reality, as God sees it, and at forming within us "the mind of Christ" (1 *Cor* 2:16). The word of God appears here as a criterion for discernment: it is "living and active, sharper than any two-edged sword, piercing to the division of soul and spirit, of joints and marrow, and discerning the thoughts and intentions of the heart" (*Heb* 4:12). We do well also to remember that the process of *lectio divina* is not concluded until it arrives at action (*actio*), which moves the believer to make his or her life a gift for others in charity.

QUESTIONS FOR REVIEW

1. Name three ways or places that Scripture is present in the Mass.
2. What is the Liturgy of the Hours?
3. What is *Lectio Divina?*
4. Name the steps involved in *Lectio Divina.*
5. What are three ways to spend more time with Jesus through the Scriptures?

QUESTIONS FOR DISCUSSION

1. Have you ever tried reading any parts of the Bible on your own? What was that experience like?
2. When you pray, do you struggle with staying focused? If so, how could incorporating more Scripture into your prayer help you overcome that?
3. What is one new way of getting to know Jesus through the Scriptures that you would be open to trying?

Part II

FROM GENESIS TO JUDGES

Overview

As we saw earlier, the first five books of the Old Testament are Genesis, Exodus, Leviticus, and Deuteronomy. The Church most commonly refers to these books as the Pentateuch, which comes from the Greek *pentateuchos*, meaning "five volumes." Sometimes, you'll also hear these books called the Torah, which is Hebrew for "instruction" or "teaching," or the Book of Moses, which refers to the tradition that says these books were written by Moses. This is how Jesus himself referenced the Pentateuch in the Gospel of Mark (12:26).

As Catholics, we believe that all the books of the Bible, these five included, have two authors: a divine author and a human author. Throughout most of Church history, scholars have followed Jesus' lead and asserted that the human author of the Pentateuch was indeed Moses, who wrote these books somewhere between the thirteenth and fifteenth centuries BC. But about two hundred years ago a new theory about the books' human authorship became popular. Often referred to as the Documentary Hypothesis, or JEDP, this theory attributed the Pentateuch not to Moses but to four different sources that contributed different documents: the Yahwist source (abbreviated as J for the German *Jahve*); the Elohist source (E); the Deuteronomist source (D); and the Priestly source (P).

Those who have argued for the Documentary Hypothesis claim that the parts of the Pentateuch attributed to J were written in the ninth or tenth century in Judah, and can be identified both by the author's use of the name YHWH for God and his narrative focus on Abraham and

David. They believe the E source was written around the ninth century in Northern Israel, and identify it by its use of the name *Elohim* for God and a textual focus on morals. The D source focuses on religious matters and temple worship, and was allegedly written around the seventh century BC. Finally, they argue that the P source was written in the fifth or sixth century BC. Its focus is on priestly matters and it is found mainly in the Book of Leviticus. Ultimately, they claim, this source was joined with the already combined J, E, and D sections.

That's the simplified version of JEDP. Depending on which scholar you read, it can get even more complicated, with multiple sub-sources contributing to each purported main source and theories that argue that both the writing and combining were influenced by competing sects and political groups.

It's important to know about the JEDP theory because many scholars still hold to it today. Nevertheless, it remains just a theory . . . and a theory with many problems and holes in it. For example, if the sources were, indeed, written at the times and places that the hypothesis maintains, then it would be very difficult for the writers to have included certain information that would have been known only in the traditional time and place of authorship (in the thirteenth or fifteenth century BC). This would include items such as native names, plants, currency rates, and covenant formats, whose accuracy has been confirmed through the study of Ancient Near Eastern texts from the time period.[1]

Moreover, the theory of JEDP itself was shaped by a number of problematic ideas, beginning with the belief, carried over from Darwin, that the more complex something is, the more recent it is. So, for example, JEDP argues that Leviticus is the newest component of the Pentateuch simply because the laws it contains are more complex. This belief, however, isn't rooted in actual fact; sometimes things simplify with the progression of time. The mere fact that Leviticus contains more complicated rules than Deuteronomy isn't proof that it's newer; it's simply more complex.

Another problematic idea underlying JEDP is anti-Semitism and

---

[1] Scott Hahn, ed., "Covenant," in *Catholic Bible Dictionary*, 171.

anti-clericalism (specifically toward Catholics). In nineteenth-century Europe, when JEDP first arose, there was a strong bias against both Jews and Catholics among the intellectual classes, who generally saw all priestly rules and duties as unnecessary to religion and an obstacle to individual freedom. Accordingly, arguing that the laws of Moses from the Priestly source were made up later (in the last stage of JEDP) and were therefore not as authentic was, for some of the theory's supporters, an attempt to invalidate early Judaism and Catholicism, both of which depend upon priests for their liturgy.

In the early twentieth century, the Pontifical Biblical Commission addressed the composition of the Pentateuch by proposing certain possibilities regarding its authorship. In the document *On the Mosaic Authorship of the Pentateuch*, it "allowed for the possibility that Moses made use of secretaries, that he may have incorporated oral and written traditions into the work, and that later scribes may have updated the work in several places to make it more intelligible to later readers."[2]

The document also explained that there was not enough evidence to discard Mosaic authorship. While the Church doesn't require Catholics to believe that Moses authored the Pentateuch, it also doesn't require Catholics to believe in JEDP or any other theory about biblical authorship other than the Church's teaching that the Bible is divinely inspired.

Ultimately, that's what matters. When it comes to the authorship of the Pentateuch and every other book in the Bible, the most important point to keep in mind is that the Scriptures are inspired by the Holy Spirit. It doesn't really matter if one man or twenty wrote the first five books of the Bible. What matters is that God inspired that writing, as well as any editing that might have gone into it and the formation of the Bible as a whole. Accordingly, we need to read and interpret all parts of Scripture in relation to the entire Bible, seeing the whole of it as one complete work, arranged by God, with purpose and intent, and seeking to prayerfully understand that purpose and intent as we read it.

---

[2] Scott Hahn, ed., "Pentateuch," in *Catholic Bible Dictionary*, 693; c.f. Dean Philip Béchard and Joseph A. Fitzmyer, *The Scripture Documents: An Anthology of Official Catholic Teachings* (Collegeville, MN: Liturgical Press, 2002), 189.

Chapter 1

THE BOOK OF GENESIS

|| ASSIGNED READING
|| Genesis 1–4; 5:1–5

In the Beginning

The word *genesis* means "origin" or "birth." The title is apt for a book that begins with the Hebrew "*bere'shit*," which means "in the beginning." It starts at the beginning of time, at the dawn of creation, relaying what is called "primeval history."

In the beginning, Genesis tells us, God created the heavens, the earth, and all they contain: the sun, the stars, the moon; the deserts and oceans, the forests and plains; lions and giraffes, bumblebees and hummingbirds. Everything that exists in creation exists because of God. This is one of the primary points of Genesis 1—to help us see that everything in creation was made by God and loved by God. "It is good," he proclaims as the world takes shape and creatures begin to walk upon it.

Then, on the sixth day, one creature—man—is greeted differently. "It is very good," God says. This man is different from the rest of creation. He is, Scripture tells us, made in the image of God.

Reflecting upon the first chapter of Genesis, the Catechism writes:

God himself created the visible world in all its richness, diversity and order. Scripture presents the work of the Creator symbolically as a succession of six days of divine "work," concluded by the "rest" of the seventh day [Gen 1:1–2:4]. On the subject of creation, the sacred text teaches the truths revealed by God for our salvation [Cf. DV 11], permitting us to "recognize the inner nature, the value and the ordering of the whole of creation to the praise of God" [LG 36 § 2]. (CCC 337)

That is to say, the purpose of Genesis isn't to teach us scientific history. It's not to explain *how* the world came to be, like a science textbook would. Rather, it's to show us *who* made the world and *why*. Genesis shows us a world created by God and a world ordered to the worship of God. It also shows us *who* we are and what makes us different from dogs and cats and parrots. Humans and humans alone are made in the image of God. Humans alone were made to have the life of God inside of us.

This is real history. It's just not the kind of history you would find in a documentary. It's more like the history depicted by a painting, one that's filled with symbolic imagery intended to convey a deeper meaning. As Peter Kreeft explains:

This does not mean that [the first part of Genesis] is myth or fable, but that its style is often poetic and that its content is selective. The author is like a photographer who points his camera only at the subjects that are important for his purposes, from his point of view.[3]

Scientific theories about how life came to be or evolved on this planet are all well and good. But none of those theories can explain the meaning and purpose of creation. They can't explain the meaning and purpose of human life. Only the Creator can do that, which is why he has given us Genesis 1—to show us who we are and for what we were made.

---

[3] Peter Kreeft, *You Can Understand the Bible* (San Francisco: Ignatius Press, 2005), 6–7.

God's Covenant with Adam

Genesis 2 sheds further light on the question by showing us the story of creation from another perspective. If Genesis 1 gives us the story of creation from thirty thousand feet, Genesis 2 gives us the story of creation from ten feet. It is the close-up of the creation story, zeroing in on the creation of man . . . or, more accurately, man and woman.

At the beginning of this narrative, we find God creating man from the ground and breathing "the breath of life"—God's own life—into him (Gen 2:7). Again, the Bible makes it clear that the human person is a being intentionally created and willed by God. It also shows us that "the human person, created in the image of God, is a being at once corporeal and spiritual" (CCC 362). This means that we are not mere spirits or mere matter, but a union of the two (CCC 365). Our bodies are us, just as our souls are us. Flesh isn't a prison our souls occupy; it's a gift from God and essential to who we are.

Genesis 2 also shows us the creation of woman, describing in figurative language how she is created as man's equal (from his side) and is as much the image of God as man. "It is not good that the man should be alone," God adds, revealing that he made us for communion with another (Gen 2:18). That is, he made us for community—both with each other and with him.

Genesis 2 also helps us see the outlines of God's first covenant with man. The terms and conditions were that man had to till (work) and keep (guard) the garden (Gen 2:15)—which is the same language used in the Old Testament to denote the work of priests and Levites—and not eat of the "tree of the knowledge of good and evil" (Gen 2:17). As long as Adam and Eve keep this commandment, they will live forever in perfect friendship with each other and with God. The biblical verse "And the man and his wife were both naked, and were not ashamed" speaks to this peace (Gen 2:25). It attests to what the Church calls "original innocence," which essentially means that our first parents were without sin. There was harmony in their relationship with one another, with God, and with all the world. Sin, sickness, and death had no place in Eden.

This changes abruptly in Genesis 3, when Satan enters the garden and tempts Adam and Eve to disobey God's command regarding the tree of the knowledge of good and evil. First Eve eats of its fruit, and then Adam does the same. With their disobedience, the original harmony of the world shatters.

This story of man and woman's fall from grace is like the story of creation itself. It is meant to be taken seriously, but not literally. The Catechism tells us:

> The account of the fall in *Genesis* 3 uses figurative language, but affirms a primeval event, a deed that took place *at the beginning of the history of man*. Revelation gives us the certainty of faith that the whole of human history is marked by the original fault freely committed by our first parents. (390)

So, here we have another painting. This painting shows us that at the dawn of human history, our first parents made a shockingly bad choice, whose consequences continue to reverberate throughout history. Sin and death, suffering and strife, all have a place in this world because humanity gave them a place.

> The account of the Fall . . . indicates that man, at the beginning of his history, rebelled against his Creator and brought sin and misery into the world. As Genesis presents it, the immediate effects of man and woman transgressing the original covenant (2:16–17) include shame (3:7), strife (3:12), suffering (3:16–19), and separation from the Lord (3:23–24). Its lasting effects, including death (3:19) and a disordered propensity toward evil (6:5), are passed down to the entire human family (CCC 390, 400).[4]

But the story doesn't end there. In Genesis 3:15, God promises Adam and Eve a redeemer. He assures them that one of their descendants will crush the head of the serpent, restoring to humanity what was lost by

---

[4] Scott Hahn and Curtis Mitch, eds., *Ignatius Catholic Study Bible: The Book of Genesis* (San Francisco: Ignatius Press, 2010), 21.

our first parents' sin. Adam failed to guard the garden; he failed to be the steward of creation that God called him to be. He chose the easy way out, sinning rather than standing up to Satan. But one day, someone would make a different choice.

From that day forward, humanity began waiting for that someone.

God's Covenant with Noah

|| ASSIGNED READING
|| Genesis 6–9:1–17; 11:1–9

While humanity waited for its redeemer, however, the state of the world only grew worse. First, Adam and Eve's eldest son Cain murdered his younger brother Abel (Gen 4:8). Cain's children, in turn, wandered far from God, and eventually the whole world was overrun by sinful, cruel people who refused to acknowledge God or walk in his ways. By the sixth chapter of Genesis there is only one man left who "walked with God": Noah, "a righteous man, blameless in his generation" (Gen 6:9).

Determined to hit the reset button on creation, God tells Noah that a flood is coming—a flood that will cover the whole earth and destroy every living thing on it. God then commands Noah to build an ark big enough to hold his family and two of every living creature, so that they survive the coming flood.

All unfolds according to God's plan, and after the flood subsides, Noah, in priestly fashion, offers a sacrifice that pleases God (Gen 8:20–22). God then establishes a covenant with Noah that includes "every living creature of all flesh" (Gen 9:15). In it, he blesses Noah and his sons, using many of the words reminiscent of the creation account with Adam and Eve. The difference between this covenant and God's first covenant with Adam is that God gives Noah permission to eat animals as well as plants. God also promises that he will never destroy the whole earth with a flood, and he sets a rainbow in the sky (v. 13) as the sign of this covenant promise. Some scholars look at the bow to represent a military bow with the curve facing the heavens as the condition of the covenant. If this was the intention, it would fit the idea of this type of covenant, in that God would be saying, "If I do not live up to my end of the deal, may I suffer the consequences" (in this case shooting an arrow at himself).

Noah resolves to honor the terms of his covenant with God, and yet, like Adam, both he and his descendants fail to do so. Sin gradually takes hold of men's hearts once more, and yet another sinful generation seeks to make a name for themselves apart from God. This time, they try to do this by building a great tower—the Tower of Babel—asserting the power of men over the world (Gen 11). God then steps in and reminds them that they have no power apart from him, confuses their language (the word for Babel comes from the Hebrew word meaning "confuse"), and scatters the people throughout the earth.

Yet again, humanity's sinful pride becomes an occasion for God to show his mercy through another covenant. Immediately after the account of Babel, Abraham is introduced. Thus, both historically and literarily, the story of Babel sets the stage for the calling of Abraham, through whom the Lord will regather the divided human race into the unity of the family of God.

The Call of Abraham

|| ASSIGNED READING
|| Genesis 12:1–9; 14:17–17:27; 22:1–19

In Genesis 12, God calls Abraham—who is still called Abram at this point—to leave his country and family to travel to a distant land. God doesn't tell Abram where he wants him to go; he simply asks Abram to begin the journey and trust that God will lead him. If Abram obeys, God promises, God will do three things for him: he will make of Abram a "great nation"; he will make Abram's "name great"; and he will bless "all the families of the earth" by Abram (Gen 12:3).

Abram could easily have dismissed these promises as impossible to fulfill. Abram was an old man, already in his mid-seventies, when God called him. He and his wife, Sarai, who was well beyond her childbearing years, had no children. They had never been able to conceive. And yet, God promised to make a great nation out of Abram's descendants. How could that be? Abram, though, was a man of faith. So, he trusts God, and in obedience sets out for this unknown land, accompanied by Sarai, his nephew Lot, and all their servants.

Eventually, Abram arrives in the land God intends for him. He builds an altar, upon which he can make a sacrifice to the Lord. Then he meets Melchizedek, the king of Salem and "priest of God Most High" (Gen 14:18). Melchizedek makes an offering of bread and wine, then blesses Abram.

In the following chapter, God appears to Abram in a vision and promises that Abram's descendants will be as numerous as the stars in the sky (15:5). This time, Abram has his doubts. "Behold, you have given me no offspring; and a slave born in my house will be my heir," he says (15:3). God reassures him that this will not happen; Abram will have a son, and that son will inherit the land that God gives to Abram.

Abram, seeking reassurance, asks, "O Lord GOD, how am I to know that I shall possess it?" (15:8). God responds by commanding Abram to bring him several animals and to cut all but a pair of birds in two. That evening, after Abram did as God commanded, "a smoking fire pot and a flaming torch passed between these pieces" (15:17). This can sound exceptionally strange and mysterious to us, but it actually reflects a specific covenant ritual, which calls for one to walk between divided animal corpses. The meaning behind it is that if one does not live up to the oath, he will call upon himself the same fate as that of the animals. So, here, God is saying much the same thing to Abram as he did to Noah: If I don't honor my promises, I will take the curse upon myself.

In Genesis 17, God revisits the second promise he made to Abram: that he would make Abram's name great. He then does the same thing he did with the first promise: he elevates it to a covenant. Not only does he swear that Abram will be the "father of a multitude of nations" from which kings will come (royal dynasty), but he also makes Abram's name literally greater; he makes it longer. "No longer shall your name be Abram, but your name shall be Abraham," he says; "for I have made you the father of a multitude of nations" (Gen 17:5).

This time there are no slaughtered animals and torches. Rather, God requires that Abraham seal the covenant with his own blood, telling Abraham that he and all his descendants must be circumcised. This signified that if one didn't live up to the covenant by being circumcised, he would be "cut off from his people" (Gen 17:14). Along with this requirement, God changes Sarai's name to Sarah, and tells her that before the year is out she will give birth to a son (Gen 17:15–21).

The Aqedah

Abraham and Sarah's son is born, just as God promised, and named Isaac. He thrives and grows, adored by both his parents. But, in Genesis 22, God tests Abraham's faith by commanding him to sacrifice Isaac. This is the *Aqedah*, which we discussed earlier.

God tells Abraham to take Isaac, his beloved son, up on Mount Moriah—which is part of a mountain range where the city of Jerusalem would one day be built—and offer him as a sacrifice. Abraham sets out to obey God. Along the way, Isaac, a young man strong enough to carry the wood of his sacrifice up the mountain, asks his father where the lamb for the sacrifice is. Abraham responds, "God will provide himself the lamb for a burnt offering" (Gen 22:8).

Isaac trusts his father to the very end, allowing his frail old father to bind his strong young body to the wood. He is, in this sense, a "type" of Christ, who also carried the wood for his sacrifice up a hill and freely submitted to the will of the Father. Unlike Jesus, though, Isaac doesn't have to die. As Abraham raises the knife to kill his son, an angel tells him to halt (Gen 22:11–12). In Isaac's stead, Abraham offers up a nearby ram—not a lamb—caught in the thicket.

According to one biblical account, Solomon would one day build his temple on that same spot where Abraham took Isaac. Likewise, Jesus would offer himself on Golgotha, one of the hills in that same chain of mountains where Abraham prepared to offer Isaac. In the end, Jesus was the lamb provided by God.

Long before Jesus came, however, immediately after Abraham shows

God the extent of his trust, God makes his third and final covenant with Abraham, upgrading his third promise to the level of a covenant, swearing that he will bless Abraham and that his descendants will be a blessing to all the nations of the world (Gen 22:18). Thousands of years later, God fulfilled that covenant when Abraham's descendent, Jesus Christ, died upon the same mountain range and brought salvation to all the world.

The Patriarchs Isaac and Jacob

> ### Assigned Reading
> Genesis 25:27–34; 27:1–40; 29:1–30:24; 32:22–32; 37,
> 41–46:7; 47:27–31; 50:15–26

Isaac, the beloved son promised to Abraham, grows up and marries a woman named Rebekah. Together, they have twin sons, Esau and Jacob. Isaac favors Esau—the hairy, masculine, and not incredibly intelligent first-born. Rebekah favors Jacob—the younger and cleverer twin (Gen 25:28).

Just as Isaac had inherited the covenantal blessing from Abraham, Esau, the firstborn son, is set to inherit the covenantal blessing from Isaac. His descendants are to be the ones who bring salvation to the world. But Esau doesn't see the true value in that blessing. He is a man of the moment, who cares about immediate pleasures and needs, so promises about future blessings matter little to him. Jacob, on the other hand, recognizes what a great gift God has given to their family and wants to be the one through whom the covenantal blessing is handed down.

Accordingly, when Jacob see the opportunity to trick Esau out of his birthright, he takes it. And he doesn't have to work very hard to do so. One day, when Esau comes home hungry, he finds Jacob cooking a pot of stew. He begs Jacob to give him some, and Jacob agrees . . . if, in exchange, Esau would give him his birthright—the right to receive the covenantal blessing. Esau willingly accepts the bargain.

Isaac, however, knows nothing of this deal. Years pass, and eventually his death approaches. At that moment, he announces his desire to hand on the blessing to Esau. Jacob (with the help of his mother) then has to trick the blessing out of his father. He deceives the old man into thinking that he is really Esau (Gen 27:18–29), and so the covenantal blessing passes to Jacob. He then leaves to live with his mother's brother Laban, rather than face the wrath of Esau (Gen 27:43–45).

In Haran, Jacob falls in love with Rachel, the daughter of Laban. Laban promises Jacob that if the young man works for him for seven years, Rachel will be his. But at the end of those seven years, the trickster finds himself tricked. Laban has disguised his eldest daughter, Leah, so that Jacob won't realize he is marrying her, not Rachel. Only on the morning after the wedding is the trick revealed. When Jacob protests, Laban promises Jacob that he will give him Rachel as well, if he agrees to work for him for another seven years. This time, Laban honors his end of the bargain.

Jacob and his wives continue to live with Laban for a number of years. In that time, Leah bears Jacob many sons, as do both her maidservant and Rachel's. Rachel, however, is unable to conceive a child. Finally, "God remembered" her, and she bears a son named Joseph (Gen 30:22–24). After living with Laban for twenty years, Jacob and his family decide to return to Canaan, Jacob's homeland. On their return journey, Jacob wrestles with a mysterious man, whom he later calls God (but whom Hosea calls an angel) (Gen 32:22–32; Hos 12:4). During the wrestling match, Jacob refuses to give up the fight until the angel blesses him. In the end, he has his way, receiving both the blessing and, like his grandfather before him, a name change. "Your name shall no more be called Jacob," the angel tells him, "but Israel, for you have striven with God and with men, and have prevailed" (Gen 32:28).

Later, in Bethel, Jacob has an encounter with God, who reaffirms the name change and the covenantal blessings he will inherit, saying, "I am God Almighty: be fruitful and multiply; a nation and a company of nations shall come from you, and kings shall spring from you. The land which I gave to Abraham and Isaac I will give to you, and I will give the land to your descendants after you" (Gen 35:11–12).

Descent into Egypt

Soon after this, Rachel dies in childbirth. The child, Benjamin, survives, making him Jacob/Israel's twelfth—and last—son (Gen 35:16–29). Of those twelve sons, Rachel's eldest, Joseph, is his father's favorite. As a sign of his favor, Jacob gives Joseph a beautiful multicolored tunic with long sleeves, which fills Joseph's brothers with envy. Joseph then makes a bad situation worse by revealing his dreams to them, dreams where his brothers' crops (as well as the sun, the moon, and eleven stars, which represented his father, mother, and brothers) bow down to him (Gen 37:6–7, 9). Even his father rebukes him for that dream.

Soon Joseph's brothers begin plotting to kill him. One brother—Reuben—convinces them instead to throw Joseph in a pit (which would allow him to go back later and rescue him), but before the plan can come to fruition, the other brothers sell Joseph into slavery. The price they receive in return is twenty shekels of silver (Gen 37:18–28).

Eventually, Joseph ends up in Egypt, where he is unjustly thrown in prison and then brought into Pharaoh's house to interpret his dreams. Based upon what Pharaoh tells him, Joseph concludes that Egypt will have seven years of abundance and then seven years of famine. Pharaoh is so impressed by Joseph that he makes him governor of Egypt (Gen 41:40–41).

During those seven years of abundance, Joseph makes sure that the Egyptians stockpile enough grain to get them through the seven years of famine that will follow. Accordingly, when famine strikes, people come from far and wide, seeking to purchase grain from the Egyptians' ample stores. Among those who come are Joseph's brothers. At their father Jacob's orders, ten of the brothers travel to Egypt. Joseph recognizes his family immediately, but they don't recognize him. Joseph takes his time, but eventually he reveals himself to them, crying tears of joy. Rather than being angry with them for what they did, he is simply overjoyed to be reunited with them. "And now do not be distressed, or angry with yourselves, because you sold me here; for God sent me before you to preserve life" (Gen 45:5).

Soon afterward, Jacob's whole family moves to Egypt at the request of Joseph (and with the permission of Pharaoh). Joseph brings his father before Pharaoh, and Jacob actually blesses Pharaoh (Gen 47:7). Jacob then remains in Egypt for seventeen years before his death (Gen 47:28). His last act before he dies is to bless all twelve of his sons. Every son receives a covenant blessing, and Judah receives the royal blessing:

> Judah, your brothers shall praise you;
>> your hand shall be on the neck of your enemies;
>> your father's sons shall bow down before you. . . .
> The scepter shall not depart from Judah,
>> nor the ruler's staff from between his feet,
> until he comes to whom it belongs;
>> and to him shall be the obedience of the peoples. (Gen
>> 49:8, 10)

After Jacob passes away, Joseph's brothers again ask him for forgiveness, fearing that now, with their father gone, he might finally seek revenge upon them for what they did to him long ago. Joseph reassures them that he has forgiven them and that he sees the hand of God in all that has transpired. "As for you, you meant evil against me; but God meant it for good, to bring it about that many people should be kept alive, as they are today" (Gen 50:20).

The Book of Genesis ends with a promise. Joseph swears to his brothers that someday their descendants will return to Canaan, the land that God gave to Abraham, Isaac, and Jacob (Gen 50:24). He then passes away. But the story isn't over. It has just begun.

That's what Genesis is about—the beginning of Salvation History, the beginning of God's plan to save his people. In the midst of a hard, cruel world, where humanity had forgotten about the God who created them and loved them, God was slowly revealing himself to a family. He was building a relationship with them—with Noah, then Abraham, Isaac, Jacob, and his twelve sons—so that he could reveal even more of himself to their descendants. He was also making them a part of his family through the covenants, binding them to him and him to them, with the blessing of the covenant passing down through the generations, so that one day that blessing could be given to all and the covenant be open to all.

SELECTED READING:
Pope Pius XII, Encyclical Concerning Some False Opinions
Threatening to Undermine the Foundations of Catholic
Doctrine *Humani Generis* (August 12, 1950), nos. 36–39

For these reasons the Teaching Authority of the Church does not
forbid that, in conformity with the present state of human sciences
and sacred theology, research and discussions, on the part of men
experienced in both fields, take place with regard to the doctrine of
evolution, in as far as it inquires into the origin of the human body
as coming from pre-existent and living matter—for the Catholic
faith obliges us to hold that souls are immediately created by God.
However, this must be done in such a way that the reasons for both
opinions, that is, those favorable and those unfavorable to evolution,
be weighed and judged with the necessary seriousness, moderation
and measure, and provided that all are prepared to submit to the
judgment of the Church, to whom Christ has given the mission of
interpreting authentically the Sacred Scriptures and of defending
the dogmas of faith. Some however, rashly transgress this liberty of
discussion, when they act as if the origin of the human body from
pre-existing and living matter were already completely certain and
proved by the facts which have been discovered up to now and by
reasoning on those facts, and as if there were nothing in the sources
of divine revelation which demands the greatest moderation and
caution in this question.

When, however, there is question of another conjectural opinion,
namely polygenism, the children of the Church by no means enjoy
such liberty. For the faithful cannot embrace that opinion which
maintains that either after Adam there existed on this earth true men
who did not take their origin through natural generation from him as
from the first parent of all, or that Adam represents a certain number
of first parents. Now it is in no way apparent how such an opinion can

be reconciled with that which the sources of revealed truth and the documents of the Teaching Authority of the Church propose with regard to original sin, which proceeds from a sin actually committed by an individual Adam and which, through generation, is passed on to all and is in everyone as his own.

Just as in the biological and anthropological sciences, so also in the historical sciences there are those who boldly transgress the limits and safeguards established by the Church. In a particular way must be deplored a certain too free interpretation of the historical books of the Old Testament. Those who favor this system, in order to defend their cause, wrongly refer to the Letter which was sent not long ago to the Archbishop of Paris by the Pontifical Commission on Biblical Studies. This letter, in fact, clearly points out that the first eleven chapters of Genesis, although properly speaking not conforming to the historical method used by the best Greek and Latin writers or by competent authors of our time, do nevertheless pertain to history in a true sense, which however must be further studied and determined by exegetes; the same chapters, (the Letter points out), in simple and metaphorical language adapted to the mentality of a people but little cultured, both state the principal truths which are fundamental for our salvation, and also give a popular description of the origin of the human race and the chosen people. If, however, the ancient sacred writers have taken anything from popular narrations (and this may be conceded), it must never be forgotten that they did so with the help of divine inspiration, through which they were rendered immune from any error in selecting and evaluating those documents.

Therefore, whatever of the popular narrations have been inserted into the Sacred Scriptures must in no way be considered on a par with myths or other such things, which are more the product of an extravagant imagination than of that striving for truth and simplicity which in the Sacred Books, also of the Old Testament, is so apparent that our ancient sacred writers must be admitted to be clearly superior to the ancient profane writers.

QUESTIONS FOR REVIEW

1. What is the purpose of the creation account in Genesis?
2. How do the opening chapters of Genesis set the stage for the rest of Salvation History?
3. What three promises did God make to Abraham?
4. What is the *Aqedah* and what does it foreshadow?
5. Who is Israel?

QUESTIONS FOR DISCUSSION

1. Like Adam, you are made in the image of God. What does that mean to you? How does it affect how you see yourself?
2. Like with Abraham, God has a plan for your life. Is it easy or difficult to trust the goodness of that plan? Why?
3. Like with Joseph, God sometimes uses our suffering and difficult situations to bring about a great good. Can you see a way in which he has done this in your life?

Chapter 2

The Book of Exodus

| ASSIGNED READING
| Exodus 1:8–12; 2–4, 7–14, 16, 20, 24, 25:1–22; 31:18–
| 33:6; 34

The Birth of Moses

The story of God's covenants continues in the Book of Exodus. "Exodus" means "going out," and here it specifically refers to the Israelites "going out" of Egypt, as Joseph had promised they would. The Egypt Jacob's descendants leave, however, is a very different Egypt than the one that Joseph governed at the end of Genesis. The Bible tells us:

> Now there arose a new king over Egypt, who did not know Joseph. And he said to his people, "Behold, the sons of Israel are too many and too mighty for us. Come, let us deal shrewdly with them." (Exod 1:8–10)

To prevent the Israelites from gaining power, the Egyptians first enslave them and then begin killing their newborn sons. One poor Israelite woman, attempting to save her child, places him in a basket (which is the same word as that used in Genesis for Noah's "ark"). She then places the basket among the reeds of the Nile river, hoping someone will find him. Someone does: Pharaoh's daughter. After rescuing the child, she names him Moses and asks a young girl, standing nearby, if she knows a woman who could help nurse him. The girl is Moses' sister, sent there by her mother to watch over her brother. She runs and fetches their mother, who then cares for Moses while he is still small.

The Call of Moses

Moses grows up in Pharaoh's household. He is wealthy, privileged, and educated as royalty. But as a young man, he loses his place in Pharaoh's family when he murders another man—an Egyptian who had been mistreating an Israelite. Moses runs away from Egypt, eventually settling in Midian, where he marries and works as a shepherd. He is already an old man when God speaks to him from a burning bush, revealing his name to Moses:

> "If I come to the sons of Israel and say to them, 'The God of your fathers has sent me to you,' and they ask me, 'What is his name?' what shall I say to them?" God said to Moses, "I AM WHO I AM." (Exod 3:13–14)

The name God reveals to Moses—also known as the Tetragrammaton, or YHWH—can't be translated with complete accuracy. According to the Catechism, the actual Hebrew phrase used in Exodus can take any number of variations, from "I AM HE WHO IS" to "I AM WHO AM" or "I AM WHO I AM" (CCC 206). Nevertheless, each of these variations reveals something similar about God. They show that he has no beginning or end because he *is*. Nobody created God, or else he would be "I am who once was not." Likewise, nobody can destroy God because then he would be "I am who will one day not be." Lastly, God's name tells us he is outside of time. His name is not "I am who was" or "I am who will be," but "I am who am." God is. He is being itself.

It's even harder to fully comprehend God's nature than it is to fully comprehend his name. But, as the Catechism reminds us, the "God, who reveals his name as 'I AM,' reveals himself as the God who is always there, present to his people in order to save them" (CCC 207). No matter what happens in the world or in our lives, God remains, eternal, unchanging, ever present.

This is what God reveals to Moses when he speaks to him from the burning bush—not just his name, but also a vital insight into his nature. Having revealed himself in this way to Moses, God then explains that he has a mission for him. Moses is to lead the Israelites out of Egypt, into the desert, for three days, so they can offer God true worship.

Moses protests. He's not good with words, he says. He can't possibly persuade Pharaoh to let the Israelites do this. So, God tells him he may use his brother, Aaron, to communicate with Pharaoh. Moses agrees, and he and Aaron go to Pharaoh to carry out their mission. But Pharaoh denies their request. Although Moses is simply asking for the people to leave Egypt for three days in order to worship, not to leave Egypt permanently, Pharaoh doesn't trust that his slaves will return.

The Ten Plagues

To help Moses persuade Pharaoh, God inflicts a series of ten plagues upon the Egyptians. After each plague, Moses offers Pharaoh the chance to change his mind. Pharaoh, however, won't back down. Finally, the time for the tenth plague arrives. If Pharaoh doesn't relent, Moses warns, the firstborn son in every household in Egypt will die. God explains the reason for this plague, saying that Israel was God's firstborn son, and "if you refuse to let him go, behold, I will slay your first-born son" (Exod 4:23).

Unlike the plagues that came before it, the tenth plague has the potential to devastate Israel as well. Their firstborn sons will not be exempt from it . . . unless they do as God commands. Before the tenth plague begins, God gives Moses specific instructions for the Israelites to follow. He tells Moses they must sacrifice an unblemished year-old male lamb, whose blood should be applied with hyssop to the doorposts of their homes, and which they must eat with bitter herbs and unleavened bread (Exod 12:5–8). If they obey these instructions, the angel of death will "pass over" their house and no harm will come upon it.

God does as he promised. All the Israelites who obeyed his command and prepared the Passover meal are spared. The Egyptians, including Pharaoh, are not. Pharaoh loses his firstborn son to the plague and, overwhelmed with grief, orders the Israelites to leave Egypt immediately, in the dead of night (Exod 12:30–32).

The Israelites don't hesitate. Already prepared for the journey, they set off straight away for the wilderness outside of Egypt. They don't know where they are going, but they don't have to know. God himself leads the way, appearing as a pillar of fire in the night and a pillar of cloud by day (Exod 13:21).

The Passover is biblical history. But it is also something more. It is an example of the "types" we talked about earlier, with the lamb foreshadowing Jesus, who is the true lamb of God, "without blemish or spot," and whose blood was shed for our salvation (1 Pet 1:19). Likewise, the Passover feast was a feast that saved; those who participated in it were spared from death. This foreshadowed another feast that saves: the Eucharist. Recall Jesus' words: "Truly, truly, I say to you, unless you eat the flesh of the Son of man and drink his blood, you have no life in you" (John 6:53). Through the Passover meal, God wasn't just saving his people from Pharaoh; he was preparing them to recognize the lamb and the feast that would save the world from spiritual death.

Escape from Egypt

Led by God, the people of Israel move swiftly out of Egypt and into the wilderness. With them, they carry the bones of Joseph, honoring his request that his body go with his people whenever they left Egypt.

It doesn't take long for Pharaoh to regret his decision. He calls up his chariots and charioteers and sets out into the wilderness with a mighty army, determined to recapture his former slaves and bring them back to Egypt. Pharaoh and his men move fast—much faster than the Israelites, with their nursing women, children, and elders. Soon, they catch up to the people, trapping them next to the waters of the Red Sea (Exod 14:5–9).

The Israelites panic and cry out against Moses. They blame him for leading them to certain death. But God intervenes. He commands Moses to stretch out his rod, and as he does, the waters of the sea part, rising up like two great walls, and the Israelites pass through (Exod 14:21–22). Undaunted, Pharaoh's army sets out to follow them, but as the last Israelite passes onto the opposite shore, Moses lowers his rod, and the waters of the Red Sea come crashing in upon the soldiers, destroying them completely.

Years later, St. Paul would explain to the Corinthians that this passage through the Red Sea was a "type" of Baptism, hinting at the salvation that would come to the world through the waters of Baptism.

> I want you to know, brethren, that our fathers were all under the cloud, and all passed through the sea, and all were baptized into Moses in the cloud and in the sea, and all ate the same supernatural food and all drank the same supernatural drink. For they drank from the supernatural Rock which followed them, and the Rock was Christ. (1 Cor 10:1–4)

Despite the miracle God performed at the Red Sea, the Israelites continue to have something of a trust problem, and as soon as they begin to grow hungry, they start complaining again, crying out against Moses and God. The Lord silences their complaints—temporarily—by sending down manna, "bread from heaven" (Exod 16:4). He also quenches their thirst with water that miraculously pours forth from a rock (Exod 17:6).

Later, in the Gospels, Jesus would present himself as the true bread from heaven (John 6:51) and as the living water (John 4:10), who would forever quench our thirst (John 4:14).

A Covenant with Israel

Several weeks after the Israelites leave Egypt, they finally arrive at the foot of Mount Sinai. It was on this mountain that God had first spoken to Moses, revealing his name and calling Moses to lead the people of Israel to freedom. And it was here that God would issue an even greater call to the Israelites.

Calling Israel his firstborn son, God announces that he wants them to be "a kingdom of priests and a holy nation," who will lead all the peoples of the world to him (Exod 19:6). He will be to Israel as a father, and they will be his children, helping the whole world to know God's name and walk in his ways.

To help them do this, he gives Moses the Ten Commandments, as well as other ordinances. The Israelites accept God's terms and his call, saying: "All the words which the LORD has spoken we will do" (Exod 24:3). The covenant is then ratified when Moses takes the blood of oxen and throws half of it on an altar and half on the people (Exod 24:6–8). This symbolizes the covenant curse: death to whomever does not hold up their end of the covenant.

After this ceremony, Moses leaves the people and goes to converse with God on the mountain. There, God carves the Ten Commandments in stone and entrusts them to Moses (Exod 31:18). He also gives Moses detailed instructions about how the Israelites are to worship God, including instructions for building a Tabernacle, making decorations for the sanctuary, priestly vestments, and other items involved in worship.

God's instructions are exceptionally detailed—so detailed that Moses' stay on the mountain lasts forty days and forty nights. During that time, the Israelites' trust issues rear their head yet again. Fearing that both Moses and God had abandoned them, they beg Aaron, Moses' brother, to make them a new god, one of gold, whom they can see and worship (Exod 32:1). Aaron complies, taking all the people's gold and melting it into a golden calf. Once the new god is on display, thousands of the Israelite people worship it. They also, the Bible tells us in Exodus 32:6, "rose up to play." This phrase suggests they were engaging in the sexually immoral acts that were part of the worship of fertility gods.

Back on the mountain, God tells Moses what is going on down below. After Moses successfully negotiates with God to prevent him from enacting the covenant curse on all his people—death—Moses heads back down the mountain. There, he witnesses the betrayal of his people, and in his anger, breaks the stone tablets upon which God had written the Ten Commandments. He then calls out: "Who is on the Lord's side? Come to me" (Exod 32:26). Only the men of the tribe of Levi respond. Moses then charges the Levites to slay every person engaged in idolatry. Some three thousand people lost their lives that day.

SELECTED READING:
St. John Chrysostom, Catechesis 3, nos. 24–27

The Israelites witnessed marvels; you also will witness marvels, greater and more splendid than those which accompanied them on their departure from Egypt.

BAPTISM & THE RED SEA

You did not see Pharaoh drowned with his armies, but you have seen the devil with his weapons overcome by the waters of baptism. The Israelites passed through the sea; you have passed from death to life. They were delivered from the Egyptians; you have been delivered from the powers of darkness. The Israelites were freed from slavery to a pagan people; you have been freed from the much greater slavery to sin.

Do you need another argument to show that the gifts you have received are greater than theirs? The Israelites could not look on the face of Moses in glory, though he was their fellow servant and kinsman. But you have seen the face of Christ in his glory. Paul cried out: *We see the glory of the Lord with faces unveiled.*

CHRIST, THE NEW MOSES

In those days Christ was present to the Israelites as he followed them, but he is present to us in a much deeper sense. The Lord was with them because of the favor he showed to Moses; now he is with us not simply because of your obedience. After Egypt they dwelt in desert places; after your departure you will dwell in heaven. Their great leader and commander was Moses; we have a new Moses, God himself, as our leader and commander.

What distinguished the first Moses? Moses, Scripture tells us, was more gentle than all who dwelt upon the earth. We can rightly say the same of the new Moses, for there was with him the very Spirit of gentleness, united to him in his inmost being. In those days Moses raised his hands to heaven and brought down manna, the bread of angels; the new Moses raises his hands to heaven and gives us the food of eternal life. Moses struck the rock and brought forth streams of water; Christ touches his table, strikes the spiritual rock of the new covenant and draws forth the living water of the Spirit. This rock is like a fountain in the midst of Christ's table so that on all sides the flocks may draw near to this living spring and refresh themselves in the waters of salvation.

GRACE & MERCY

Since this fountain, this source of life, this table surrounds us with untold blessings and fills us with the gifts of the Spirit, let us approach it with sincerity of heart and purity of conscience to receive grace and mercy in our time of need. Grace and mercy be yours from the only-begotten Son, our Lord and Savior Jesus Christ; through him and with him be glory, honor and power to the Father and the life-giving Spirit, now and always and for ever. Amen.

QUESTIONS FOR REVIEW

1. What name did God reveal to Moses and what did it mean?
2. What was different about the tenth plague God sent upon Egypt?
3. What event in Exodus prefigured the Eucharist? Explain.
4. What event in Exodus prefigured Baptism? Explain.
5. What did God promise Israel in the covenant he made with them at Mount Sinai?

QUESTIONS FOR DISCUSSION

1. When God called Moses to go before Pharaoh, Moses didn't believe he was equipped to answer that call. Have you ever felt like God was asking you to do something you weren't prepared to do? Explain.
2. On their journey from Egypt to Sinai, God provided for Israel's needs. How does God provide for your needs?
3. Rather than worship the true God, the Israelites made an idol out of gold and worshipped that instead. What "idols" do we see people put before God sometimes?

Chapter 3

The Books of Leviticus, Numbers, and Deuteronomy

> **ASSIGNED READING**
> Leviticus 16:20–22; 18:1–5; 19:17–18; 20:2–26
> Numbers 13–14, 25
> Deuteronomy 6–9, 29, 31–36

A New Law, A New Priesthood

All those slain at the foot of Mount Sinai encountered the same divine wrath encountered by those who lost their lives in the Flood and those who were scattered and confused in Babel. They were trying to live life apart from God, and they suffered the consequences of that decision. But God had called Israel to be his own people. He had a special mission for them. They were the people he was preparing to receive the gift of his Son. Therefore, their decision to break their covenant promises didn't change their mission; it just changed how God was going to prepare them.

Originally, God intended every firstborn male to be a priest. After their "fall" at Mount Sinai, however, only those who had rallied to Moses' side—the Levites—would be ministers of worship. Likewise, the covenant law first given at Sinai was a fairly straightforward law; after their fall, God would give them a new law, a lower law, to obey. This lower law was symbolized by the new set of Ten Commandments Israel received. The Commandments were the same, but while God himself carved the first set in stone, Moses carved the second set. Much of the lower law itself is contained in the Book of Leviticus, which takes its name from the newly priestly caste, the Levites.

The Book of Leviticus is divided into two main sections. The first section, made up of the Priestly Code (Lev 1–16), served as a guidebook to teach and prepare the Levitical priests as they carried out their new duties. The second part, the Holiness Code (Lev 17–27), was for the entire nation of Israel and showed them what it meant to live as God's holy people, set apart from other nations.

When people decide to read the Bible cover to cover, Leviticus is where many of them often stop. Up until Leviticus, most of the Bible is a narrative, recounting the lives of the patriarchs. Then, with the construction of the Tabernacle (the mobile worship tent used by the Israelites in the desert), the Book of Exodus ends and Leviticus begins. What follows—lengthy and detailed rules about animal sacrifice, Sabbath observances, and more—is decidedly less interesting for the new reader, and so many give up. When you understand what and who Leviticus is for, though, it makes for better study. Nevertheless, when approaching the Bible for the first time, it's often easier to continue straight on from Exodus to the Book of Numbers, where the narrative picks up once more.

On the Edge of the Promised Land

The Book of Numbers takes us to the edge of the Promised Land, the land promised by God to Abraham and his descendants and which they had left long ago to travel to Egypt in the time of famine. Centuries had passed since then, and the land was inhabited by the Canaanites, a people who did not worship the One True God or follow his ways. Taking back the land from the Canaanites was to be the first order of business upon the Israelites' entrance into the Promised Land. God tells Moses not to worry. He will deliver the land into their hands. He has a plan.

The first part of that plan requires that Moses send twelve spies ahead of the people. Their task is to enter Canaan and gain valuable information about the land and its inhabitants (Num 13). Ten of the spies don't like what they see. When they return, they tell the Israelites that the Canaanites are too big and too strong to defeat in battle. Forgetting about God's promise to deliver the land into their hands, they conclude that entering Canaan is an impossible task. Two of the spies—Joshua and Caleb—try to convince the Israelites that they have nothing to fear, but the people refuse to listen to them. Once more, they break faith with God, crying out:

> "Would that we had died in the land of Egypt! Or would that we had died in this wilderness! Why does the LORD bring us into this land, to fall by the sword? Our wives and our little ones will become a prey; would it not be better for us to go back to Egypt?" And they said to one another, "Let us choose a captain, and go back to Egypt." (Num 14:2–4)

For their lack of faith, the entire nation is punished. The ten fearful spies die immediately (Num 14:36–37). The rest of the people—save for Joshua and Caleb—are condemned to wander in the wilderness for another forty years, until every adult Israelite has passed away (Num 14:22–24).

The Second Law

The Book of Deuteronomy finds the Israelites once more at the edge of the Promised Land. Moses has reached the end of his life, and the Israelites have reached the end of their desert wanderings. A new generation of Israelites—the children of those who came out of Egypt—are preparing to enter and finally take hold of their inheritance. Before they do, the dying Moses has something to say to them.

At the end of the Book of Numbers, the second generation of Israelites proved themselves no better than the first. They betrayed God and worshipped the false god Baal at Peor. Forty years earlier, when their parents had broken their covenant with God on Mount Sinai, God gave them a new and lower law, a law that was more suited to their "stiff-necked" and "hard hearted" ways. Now, before they can enter Canaan, he does the same, both renewing his covenant with his people and giving them yet another, even lower law to guide them as they begin life in a new land.

On the plains of Moab, Moses instructs the people that they must live in total fidelity to the Lord. He then gives them detailed covenant stipulations: the sanctions, blessings, and curses that will come with obedience or disobedience. The law Moses gives to them includes several concessions—such as permission to war against their enemies and permission for men to divorce their wives. God made these concessions, Jesus later explains, because he knew the Israelites weren't capable of doing any better. "For your hardness of heart Moses allowed you to divorce your wives, but from the beginning it was not so" (Matt 19:8). In other words, God was trying to make it easier, not harder, for the Israelites to keep the covenants.

It's not just the law that is given, however, that is lower in Deuteronomy (which literally means "Second Law"). The covenant renewal ceremony that takes place is also watered down. On Mount Sinai, God himself spoke to his people as the covenant was made. On the plains of Moab, he speaks through Moses.

The Pentateuch ends with the death of Moses, who is not allowed to enter into the Promised Land because he, too, had failed to trust in the Lord at one point in the Israelites' desert wanderings (Num 20:10–13). So, before his death, Moses prepares Joshua to take his place as the leader of his people, and then he passes away on the edge of the Promised Land (Deut 34:5).

SELECTED READING:
Curtis J. Mitch, "Divine Revelation: How God's Plan Is
Known by Us," in *Catholic for a Reason: Scripture and the
Mystery of the Family of God*, pp. 60–62

The third characteristic of divine Revelation involves our response.
When God offers Himself to His people, He expects us to embrace
Him and give our full assent to His plan. God wants nothing less
from us than the "obedience of faith" (Rom. 1:5; 16:26). After all,
God is our Creator and He alone knows what is best for us and what
is profitable for leading us to heaven. The New Testament teaches
that "without faith it is impossible to please him. For whoever would
draw near to God must believe that he exists and that he rewards
those who seek him" (Heb. 11:6). A living faith, then, is required of
those who receive God's Revelation directly or as it is handed on. We
saw above that Revelation was always given to facilitate our salvation. To reject God and turn our backs on His will is foolishness; we
would only endanger our souls and subject ourselves to God's just
punishment.

The Bible is full of such warnings about the dangers of rebellion.
One example stands out. When God rescued Israel from slavery in
Egypt, He brought them safely into the wilderness and wished to give
them the Promised Land. To ensure that Israel's gratitude and commitment were sincere, God put the nation to the test. He requested
that twelve spies inspect Canaan and bring back a report to the Israelites. As it turned out, Canaan was a dangerous-looking place, and
the inhabitants were powerful and numerous. Ten of the twelve
spies declined God's offer to enter Canaan. They even convinced the
people that God's plan was senseless and dangerous. Only two spies,
Joshua and Caleb, stepped out in faith. They alone trusted that God
would protect His people in spite of the odds. God, for His part, had
to respond to Israel's faithlessness with justice and punishment. He
swore an oath that no one of that generation would ever see Canaan,
except Joshua and Caleb (cf. Num. 14:20–24). The Israelites were
thus condemned to wander aimlessly for forty years in the wilder-

ness and eventually die. The Book of Hebrews recalls this episode to warn the early Christians to steer clear of unbelief and disobedience. The author speaks of the Israelites when he says, "[T]he message which they heard did not benefit them, because it did not meet with faith in the hearers" (Heb. 4:2).

Conversely, God rewards His faithful and obedient children. Like Joshua and Caleb, the righteous will receive God's promises and inherit the eternal homeland, heaven itself. When Abraham trusted that God would bless him with a son, the Lord "reckoned it to him as righteousness" (Gen. 15:6). Zechariah and Elizabeth, the parents of John the Baptist, were also blessed by God for their fidelity to His law. According to Luke, they "were both righteous before God, walking in all the commandments and ordinances of the Lord blameless" (Lk. 1:6). Divine Revelation is a divine invitation: God the Father wants His children to respond to Him with heartfelt love and gratitude.

QUESTIONS FOR REVIEW

1. Before the incident of the golden calf in Exodus, who among the Israelites did God intend to become priests? Who became priests after the incident of the golden calf? Why?
2. What is contained in the first half of the Book of Leviticus? What is contained in the second half of the Book of Leviticus?
3. Why and how are the Israelites punished when they finally reach the Promised Land in the Book of Numbers?
4. What does "Deuteronomy" mean?
5. How is the law given in Deuteronomy a "lower law" than the law given at Sinai?

QUESTIONS FOR DISCUSSION

1. Have you ever disobeyed your parents and had them respond by establishing stricter rules? Why do you think that was their response?
2. Why do you think God had to give Israel such specific laws in Leviticus? How was he like a father to them in how he responded?
3. Why, after all he had done for them, do you think the Israelites refused to trust God when they reached the Promised Land? Do you ever find yourself struggling to trust God in a similar way?

Chapter 4

JOSHUA AND THE JUDGES

ASSIGNED READING
Joshua 1–2, 6, 11:16–24; 21:41–43; 23, 24
Judges 2, 4–6, 13–16
Ruth 1–4

Homecoming

Deuteronomy ends with the Israelites prepared to seize control of the land of Canaan as their inheritance. The Book of Joshua begins with the first victory in that quest.

Like Moses before him, Joshua sends spies to Jericho (Josh 2). Once he has the information he needs, he leads Israel, carrying the Ark of the Covenant (which contained Israel's greatest sacred treasures and represented the presence of God among them). They then cross the Jordan River, which parts as the Red Sea once did. Upon reaching the other side, he has all the men circumcised and celebrates the Passover. Then, upon God's command, they march around the city of Jericho once a day for six days. On the seventh day, the Israelites march around the city seven times with the Ark of the Covenant carried by priests, with seven priests blowing seven horns. On the seventh circuit, the men shout, and the walls of Jericho come down (Josh 6:20). The Israelites then conquer the city, taking all the precious metal for the Lord's treasury (Josh 6:19).

With Jericho secured, Joshua continues to conquer kings and territories within the Promised Land, one by one. As he does, he distributes the land among the twelve tribes of Israel. The Levites are given cities instead of land.

The conquest of Canaan continues throughout the Book of Judges. Although the original plan isn't for the conquest to take generations, the Israelites have a bad habit of disobeying God. After Joshua's death, they fall back into their old sinful ways. They stop depending on God, start depending on themselves, and invariably find themselves defeated by their enemies. When this would happen, Israel would eventually wise up, repent, and beg God to help them—which he always would.

To deliver them from their enemies, God would then raise up a strong leader—a judge—who would lead them to victory in battle. The Israelites would rejoice, enjoying the time of peace . . . and then eventually relapse into their old ways, forgetting God once more, and the cycle would start all over again with a new judge.

> Whenever the Lord raised up judges for them, the Lord was with the judge, and he saved them from the hand of their enemies all the days of the judge; for the Lord was moved to pity by their groaning because of those who afflicted and oppressed them. But whenever the judge died, they turned back and behaved worse than their fathers, going after other gods, serving them and bowing down to them. (Judg 2:18–19)

The root of all this rebellion is the Israelites' failure to take the land God had promised them from the Canaanites. Not only do they repeatedly not trust God's promises to help them in battle—promises which he more than makes good on every time he raises up a new judge—but they also forsake him, committing idolatry by worshipping the deities of the Canaanites. Division also arises among the tribes, sparking civil war and leading the people to cry out to God for a king. All the other nations surrounding them had kings, and Israel thought if they had one too, all their troubles would end, and they would be just like the other nations: wealthy, powerful, and united.

Ruth

In the midst of all this unfaithfulness, the Bible gives us one account of true faithfulness: the Book of Ruth. Ruth lives in the time of the Judges. She is not an Israelite; rather, she belongs to a different people and had married an Israelite. After he passes away, her Israelite mother-in-law, Naomi, wants to return to her people in Canaan. Naomi has lost everything while living in a foreign land—her husband and both of her sons. Ruth, out of love for her mother-in-law, makes sure Naomi doesn't lose her too:

> Entreat me not to leave you or to return from following you; for where you go I will go, and where you lodge I will lodge; your people shall be my people, and your God my God; where you die I will die, and there will I be buried. (Ruth 1:16–17)

God blesses both of them for Ruth's faithfulness. Ruth marries Boaz, and their child, Obed, becomes the grandfather of King David (Ruth 4:13, 17). Naomi, in turn, has a new family to love and is remembered and honored as a faith-filled woman in a faithless time.

SELECTED READING:
Father Joseph L. Ponessa, S.S.D., Sharon Doran, M.A., and Laurie Manhardt, "The Book of Judges," in *The Rise and Fall of Ancient Israel*, pp. 24–25

Israel Plays the Harlot

The time of the judges reveals this one main theme throughout the entire book. Because the individual tribes are unsuccessful at completely driving out the enemy nations, Israel becomes indoctrinated with foreign gods, and falls into idolatry. Their own religion and moral compass often seems nonexistent. The great harlotry of Israel leads to great spiritual weakness.

Joshua leads the Israelites into the Promised Land, giving them the courage to follow God's commands and to fight off their seven deadly enemies, namely the Hittites, Girgashites, Amorites, Canaanites, Perizzites, Hivites, and Jebusites, seven nations mightier and more numerous than the new Joshua generation of Israel (Deuteronomy 7:1). Church fathers compare the seven deadly nations to the seven deadly sins that each Christian must continue to battle in their own journey toward the Promised Land of heaven. If sin isn't fully eradicated, we, too, run the risk of repeated sin cycles as experienced by the Israelites. The Book of Judges contains seven repeated cycles of sin, which cause Israel to spiral downward into great spiritual darkness. The perfection of the sin cycle in Judges looks like the following diagram, repeated seven times throughout the book. God, as loving husband, continually provides Judges to periodically deliver His chosen bride throughout each progressive sin cycle over the three hundred thirty year period.

Because Israel does not keep the commands of the Lord, great moral relativism creeps into their culture: *"every man did what was right in his own eyes"* (Judges 17:6b). Cardinal Joseph Ratzinger (Pope Emeritus Benedict XVI) delivered a homily before the conclave convened to replace the deceased Pope John Paul II. Cardinal Ratzinger noted a similarity between modern culture and what had happened at the time of the Judges when *everyone did what was right in his own eyes.*

> Relativism, that is, letting oneself be *tossed here and there, carried about by every wind of doctrine,* seems the only attitude that can cope with modern times. We are building *a dictatorship of relativism* that does not recognize anything as definitive and whose ultimate goal consists solely of one's own ego and desires.

QUESTIONS FOR REVIEW

1. Who was the new leader of the Israelites after Moses?
2. Who were the Judges?
3. What command of God's did Israel continually fail to obey and how did that contribute to their troubles?
4. In what way did Israel want to be like other nations?
5. Who was one of Ruth's descendants?

QUESTIONS FOR DISCUSSION

1. The Israelites had a bad habit of falling again and again into the same sins. Do you ever find yourself with a similar struggle? Why do you think this is?
2. The Israelites longed to be like other nations and envied the things those nations had. What do you think the Israelites didn't see about the goodness of their own situation?
3. The Israelites' envy often led them away from God. How can wanting the things of the world lead us away from God? Have you ever been in a situation where you chose the things the world says are important over the things God says is important? Explain.

Part III

Rise and Fall: From Samuel to Maccabees

At the very beginning of Israel's history, God had promised Abraham that kings would be numbered among his descendants. The Historical Books show us how the Lord honored that promise, recounting the rise and fall of the Davidic kingdom.

Unlike the Pentateuch, which progresses in strictly chronological terms, much of the material in the historical books overlaps. The writers of the different books often write about the same people, places, and events, looking at them from different angles. For example, 2 Samuel and 1 Chronicles both tell the story of King David's rule. 2 Samuel, however, focuses on how David made Israel into a mighty kingdom, while 1 Chronicles focuses on how David revitalized the liturgical life of Israel. In some ways, it's like reading two different books about the American Revolution, one that focuses on the military battles and another that focuses on the political battles. Both perspectives are important and accurate, but they are still different.

All together, these historical books span a time period of more than eight hundred years. They are:

- **1 and 2 Samuel**, which cover events from the end of the time of the Judges (ca. 1020 BC) to the end of David's life (ca. 970 BC);
- **1 and 2 Kings**, which begin with the last days of David and end with the Babylonian Exile and the destruction of the Temple (586 BC);
- **1 and 2 Chronicles**, which begin with the end of King Saul's reign (ca. 1010 BC) and end with the return of the people from exile in Babylon (538 BC);

- **Ezra and Nehemiah**, which focus on the reorganization of the Jewish community after the Babylonian Exile (458–430 BC);
- **1 and 2 Maccabees**, which address the challenges the Jewish people faced under later oppressors, including the Greeks (168–142 BC);
- **Esther**, which tells one specific story about the plight of the Jews in Babylon and how they were rescued from death by a Jewish woman married to a pagan king during the fourth or fifth century BC;
- **Tobit**, which recalls the troubles of an Israelite family living in exile after the fall of Northern Israel to the Assyrians;
- **Judith**, which tells the dramatic tale of how one woman delivered her people from an evil ruler; it is most likely set at some point during the fifth or sixth century.

Chapter 1

FIRST AND SECOND SAMUEL

||| ASSIGNED READING
||| 1 Samuel 2, 3, 5–8, 9, 12, 15, 16, 17, 24, 31
||| 2 Samuel 5–7, 11–12, 23, 24

The Last of the Judges

The First Book of Samuel begins with the story of Hannah, a righteous Israelite woman who is unable to have children. Year after year, Hannah begs the Lord for a baby, but no baby comes. Finally, one day, while she is praying and weeping in the temple, the priest Eli hears her. At first, he thinks she is drunk, but when she explains her problem, Eli assures her that God will hear her prayer (1 Sam 1:17). And sure enough, Hannah soon conceives a son, Samuel, whom God raises up to be the last judge of Israel.

Samuel is a good and wise judge, but in his old age, he makes a grave mistake. Rather than trust the Lord to raise up a new judge after him, Samuel appoints his sons to succeed him. Neither son is as good or as wise as their father, and the people resent their leadership. Moreover, the people are tired of judges; they want a king like all the other nations. They don't think the judges, who rule in God's stead, are good enough for them. Only a king like other nation's kings will do.

At first, Samuel protests. But in prayer God speaks to him, saying, "Listen to the voice of the people in all that they say to you; for they have not rejected you, but they have rejected me from being king over them" (1 Sam 8:7).

The Lord then leads Samuel to Saul—a tall and handsome man, who is the very picture of what the people think a king should be. Samuel, in his role as a priest, anoints Saul with oil, which signifies that Saul is now God's chosen king, one who rules by divine favor. As the anointed one, Saul is entrusted with protecting the Israelite people. He also is entrusted with ensuring that they continue to walk in God's ways. On the first count, Saul does not disappoint; he immediately leads the people to victory in battle against the Ammonites (1 Sam 11). On the second count, however, Saul fails miserably, succumbing to pride and disobeying God's commands.

As punishment for Saul's sins, God takes the throne away from him and sends Samuel to anoint a new king, a king who will be "a man after [God's] own heart" (1 Sam 13:14).

King David

That man after God's own heart is David, the youngest son of Jesse. When Samuel finds him, David is still a young man, living at home and tending his father's sheep. Samuel anoints him there on the spot (1 Sam 16:13). Yet it would be many years before David would become king. For a time, Saul would continue to reign, although without God's favor. In the meantime, David goes on to deliver Israel from the Philistine giant, Goliath, slaying him with a stone from his slingshot and proving that strength and military might are no match for God's help (1 Sam 17). David also becomes close friends with Saul's son, Jonathan, and for a time is a favorite of the king.

Once David begins assisting Saul in battle and winning far more victories than the king, that changes. Saul realizes that David is a threat to his throne and does all he can to stop David's rise to power. But no matter how close Saul's men come to capturing David and taking his life, David always escapes. David also shows nothing but respect for Saul, even refusing to take Saul's life when he has the opportunity, because Saul, too, had been God's anointed one (1 Sam 24 and 26).

After Saul dies in battle, falling on his own sword (1 Sam 31:4), his army proclaims his son Ishbosheth king of Israel. But the tribe of Judah declares David their king. Civil war ensues. Finally, Abner, the captain of Ishbosheth's army, switches sides and declares his loyalty to David. Soon after, the civil war ends and David is crowned king of Israel. He is just thirty years old.

One of David's first acts as king is to establish his capital in the city of Jerusalem. This, however, requires another military campaign. Although the Israelites controlled most of their ancestral land, the Jebusites (a Canaanite tribe) still controlled Jerusalem. In short order, God delivers the city into David's hands, and David sets about rebuilding the city, making it into the political and religious center of Israel.

To do the former, David asks his friend King Hiram of Tyre to send his Phoenician craftsmen to Jerusalem, to help him build his palace and other buildings. To do the latter, David brings the Ark of the Covenant to Jerusalem. The Ark was Israel's most precious treasure, signifying God's presence among them. Made of acacia wood and gold (according to exacting instructions given by God to Moses on Mount Sinai), it contained the Ten Commandments, carved in stone by Moses, plus Aaron's rod and manna from Israel's wilderness wanderings. David knew that giving the Ark a new home in Jerusalem would solidify the capital as the center of national life.

However, David's first attempt to bring the Ark to his capital city fails. Although Moses left strict instructions that the Ark was only to be carried by the Levites, and touched by no one else, David attempts to transport the Ark by cart (2 Sam 6:3). Not only does the cart become stuck on a road, but one of the people transporting it (who is not a Levite) dies when he touches it. At this point, David decides he needs to take Moses' instructions seriously. He brings in the Levites, who carry the Ark into Jerusalem. While they walk, David dances alongside them, leaping with joy that the Ark has finally come home (2 Sam 6:14–15).

A Kingdom of God

Although David's military and political accomplishments are great and important, equally important is the work he does to renew Israel's liturgical life. He is the primary contributor and inspiration behind the Psalms, the great liturgical songs of Israel. Likewise, a thanksgiving sacrifice of bread and wine—called the *todah*—becomes one of the most significant rituals in ancient Israel. David himself remains a man after God's own heart, sinning grievously at times, but always sincerely repenting and then seeking to glorify God.

What David wants to do most of all, though, is build God a temple. David thinks it is wrong that he lives in a "house of cedar" while the Ark dwells in a tent (2 Sam 7:2). But God has different plans and, through the prophet Nathan, explains that it will be David's son Solomon, not David himself, who would build God a temple. As for David, Nathan continues, God will make a covenant with him and his descendants. The seven promises of that covenant include:

1. I will make for you a great name. . . .
2. I will raise up your offspring after you, who shall come forth from your body, and I will establish his kingdom.
3. He shall build a house for my name, . . .
4. I will establish the throne of his kingdom for ever.
5. I will be his father, and he shall be my son.
6. When he commits iniquity, I will chasten him . . . ; but I will not take my merciful love from him, as I took it from Saul. . . .
7. And your house and your kingdom shall be made sure for ever before me; your throne shall be established for ever. (2 Sam 7:9, 12–16)

All those promises boil down to one: Through David's offspring, God will establish an everlasting kingdom—a kingdom that will be ruled by one that God describes as his "son." This covenant, David himself says, will be an "everlasting covenant" (2 Sam 23:5). It will endure forever, despite his sins and despite his children's sins.

SELECTED READING:
Saint Augustine of Hippo, *City of God*, bk. 17, ch. 8[1]

When many things had gone prosperously with king David, he thought to make a house for God, even that temple of most excellent renown which was afterwards built by king Solomon his son. While he was thinking of this, the word of the Lord came to Nathan the prophet, which he brought to the king, in which, after God had said that a house should not be built unto Him by David himself, and that in all that long time He had never commanded any of His people to build Him a house of cedar. He says, "And now thus shall you say unto my servant David, Thus says God Almighty, '. . . And it shall come to pass when your days be fulfilled, and you shall sleep with your fathers, that I will raise up your seed after you, which shall proceed out of your bowels, and I will prepare his kingdom. He shall build me a house for my name; and I will order his throne even to eternity. I will be his Father, and he shall be my son. And if he commit iniquity, I will chasten him with the rod of men, and with the stripes of the sons of men: but my mercy I will not take away from him, as I took it away from those whom I put away from before my face. And his house shall be faithful, and his kingdom even for evermore before me, and his throne shall be set up even for evermore.'"

He who thinks this grand promise was fulfilled in Solomon greatly errs; for he attends to the saying, "He shall build me a house," but he does not attend to the saying, "His house shall be faithful, and his kingdom for evermore before me." Let him therefore attend and behold the house of Solomon full of strange women worshipping false gods, and the king himself, aforetime wise, seduced by them, and cast down into the same idolatry: and let him not dare to think that God either promised this falsely, or was unable to foreknow that Solomon and his house would become what they did. But we ought not to be in doubt here, or to see the fulfillment

---

[1] Augustine, *The City of God*, vols. I and II, edited by Anthony Uyl (London: T&T Clark, 1871, repr., Ontario, CN: Devoted Publishing, 2017).

of these things save in Christ our Lord, who was made of the seed of David according to the flesh, lest we should vainly and uselessly look for some other here . . .

For even [the Jewish people] understand this much, that the son whom they read of in that place as promised to David was not Solomon . . . Indeed, even in Solomon there appeared some image of the future event, in that he built the temple, and had peace according to his name (for Solomon means pacific), and in the beginning of his reign was wonderfully praiseworthy; but while, as a shadow of Him that should come, he foreshowed Christ our Lord, he did not also in his own person resemble Him. Whence some things concerning him are so written as if they were prophesied of himself, while the Holy Scripture, prophesying even by events, somehow delineates in him the figure of things to come.

For, besides the books of divine history, in which his reign is narrated, the 72nd Psalm also is inscribed in the title with his name, in which so many things are said which cannot at all apply to him, but which apply to the Lord Christ with such evident fitness as makes it quite apparent that in the one the figure is in some way shadowed forth, but in the other the truth itself is presented. For it is known within what bounds the kingdom of Solomon was enclosed; and yet in that psalm, not to speak of other things, we read, "He shall have dominion from sea even to sea, and from the river to the ends of the earth," which we see fulfilled in Christ. Truly he took the beginning of His reigning from the river where John baptized; for, when pointed out by him, He began to be acknowledged by the disciples, who called Him not only Master, but also Lord.

QUESTIONS FOR REVIEW

1. Who was the last judge of Israel?
2. Who was the first king of Israel?
3. Where did David establish his capital city?
4. Name two liturgical developments that occurred under King David.
5. What promise was at the heart of God's covenant with David?

QUESTIONS FOR DISCUSSION

1. The prophet Samuel didn't trust God to appoint his successor and took it upon himself to do so. Negative consequences followed. Can you think of a time you failed to trust God and something bad happened? Explain.
2. Even though God told Israel they were special because he—not a human being—was their king, the Israelites still wanted a human king like all the other nations. Have you ever wanted something that was bad or less than ideal, simply because you wanted to be like everybody else? What happened? Explain.
3. David wanted to build God a temple, but God had different and better plans. Have you ever wanted to do something that didn't work out, only to discover that God had something better in store for you? Explain.

Chapter 2

First and Second Kings

 ‖ Assigned Reading
 ‖ 1 Kings 3, 9, 11–14, 18, 22
 ‖ 2 Kings 1, 2, 17–19, 21–25

The Son of David

At first, God's promise to David—that his kingdom would last forever—seems perfectly straightforward. At the time of David's death, his kingdom is great. After his son Solomon ascends to the throne, it becomes even greater.

The growing strength of Israel is made possible in large part by a gift God gives to Solomon early in his reign. After David's death the Lord speaks to Solomon and says, "Ask what I shall give you" (1 Kgs 3:5). Solomon responds, "Give your servant therefore an understanding mind to govern your people, that I may discern between good and evil" (1 Kgs 3:9). God answers Solomon's request, giving Solomon a wisdom that surpasses that of any other man or woman. People come from far and wide to learn from him, and Israel's reputation as a great nation spreads.

God's promise that Solomon would build him a temple also soon comes to pass. The temple takes seven years to build and is dedicated on the seventh month of the year. The Ark of the Covenant is brought inside, and the presence of the Lord is among them (1 Kgs 8:10–11). In his prayer of dedication, Solomon asks God to be with his people even if they should disobey. He also includes the following prayer:

> Likewise when a foreigner, who is not of your people Israel, comes from a far country for your name's sake (for they shall hear of your great name, and your mighty hand, and of your outstretched arm), when he comes and prays toward this house, hear in heaven your dwelling place, and do according to all for which the foreigner calls to you; in order that all the peoples of the earth may know your name and fear you, as do your people Israel, and that they may know that this house which I have built is called by your name. (1 Kgs 8:41–43)

Through this prayer, Solomon is showing that his temple is not only for Israel, but for all people. This marks a sea change in how Israel dealt with other nations. On Mount Sinai, God had told his people that he wanted them to be a light to other nations and to help all the people of the earth walk in God's ways. But then the Israelites showed themselves incapable of answering that call. They were too easily influenced *by* the world to have a positive influence *on* the world. From that point forward, God commanded Israel to remain separate from other nations. He kept them apart so that he could better form them. Solomon's prayer signifies that, at long last, Israel is ready to start doing what it was always supposed to do. The time had come for them to be the witness to the world that God had always meant them to be.

Or had it?

After hearing Solomon's prayer, God responds to him, saying:

> I have heard your prayer and your supplication, which you have made before me; I have consecrated this house which you have built, and put my name there for ever. . . . And as for you, if you will walk before me, as David your father walked, with integrity of heart and uprightness, doing according to all that I have commanded you, and keeping my statutes and my ordinances, then I

will establish your royal throne over Israel for ever. . . . But if you . . . do not keep my commandments and my statutes which I have set before you, but go and serve other gods and worship them, then I will cut off Israel from the land which I have given them; and the house which I have consecrated for my name I will cast out of my sight; and Israel will become a proverb and a byword among all peoples. (1 Kgs 9:3–7)

Sure enough, Solomon, like so many of his ancestors before him, fails. To strengthen his kingdom, he marries countless women—the daughters of foreign kings. Eventually, he begins building temples to their gods too. He taxes his people heavily, and fails to teach his son and heir, Rehoboam, what it means to rule wisely and faithfully. All the great wisdom God had given Solomon was given so that he could build a kingdom for God. Instead, Solomon built a kingdom for himself. And like all things of this world, it didn't last.

Collapse

After Solomon's death, Rehoboam taxes the people heavily to subsidize his lavish lifestyle, and in protest, ten of Israel's twelve tribes rebel. They separate from him, name another man, Jeroboam, their king, and form a new kingdom, which they continue to call Israel. Only two tribes remain with the house of David in the south: the small tribe of Benjamin and the large tribe of Judah. The Southern Kingdom takes the larger tribe's name and becomes known as Judah.

Not surprisingly, the leader of the Northern Kingdom, Jeroboam, proves no better than Rehoboam. Cruel and godless, he offers sacrifices to two golden calves (1 Kgs 12:32), just as his ancestors did on Mount Sinai. At the same time, as the people increasingly turn their back on God in the Northern Kingdom of Israel, something similar begins to happen in the Southern Kingdom of Judah: the people forget God's ways and worship false gods. Eventually, a series of kings, both in the north and in the south, go to war against each other (1 Kgs 15–16).

Through it all, however, God is patient. Over the course of two hundred years, he sends many prophets to the people. The prophets call the Israelites to repent and return to the Lord; yet, in the north, most don't listen. Finally, in 722 BC, Israel falls to the Assyrians. Many of the land's inhabitants are sent into exile, never to be heard from again. Others are killed, while only a few remain in northern Israel, intermarrying with the foreigners brought in by Assyria. All that is distinctive about them, as tribes and a people, is lost.

The Second Book of Kings explains:

> And this was so, because the sons of Israel had sinned against the LORD their God . . . and had feared other gods and walked in the customs of the nations whom the LORD drove out before the sons of Israel. . . . They built for themselves high places at all their towns, from watchtower to fortified city; they set up for themselves pillars; . . . they burned incense on all the high places. . . . they did wicked things, . . . they served idols. . . . Yet the LORD warned Israel and Judah by every prophet and every seer, saying, "Turn from your evil ways and keep my commandments and my statutes. . . ." But they would not listen. . . . They despised his statutes, and his covenant that he made with their fathers. . . . Therefore the LORD was very angry with Israel. (2 Kgs 17:7–15, 18)

In the Southern Kingdom of Judah, the people fare somewhat better. Although many kings as cruel and godless as Jeroboam come to rule over them, two kings at least try to bring their people back to the Lord. First Hezekiah and then Josiah, both descendants of King David, attempt to restore right worship. Josiah is the most successful, primarily because the high priest, Hilkiah, finds the lost book of Deuteronomy (called the Book of the Law) while making repairs on the temple. After making inquiries about the book, Josiah concludes it is the true word of God and calls the people to obey it (2 Kgs 22:11–13).

After their king reads the Book of the Law to them, all the people in Judah swear to obey its commands. At the king's orders, all the altars to pagan gods are burned, and all foreign religious practices banned. Josiah even reintroduces the celebration of the Passover. Of him, the Bible says, "Before him there was no king like him, who turned to the LORD with all his heart and with all his soul and with all his might" (2 Kgs 23:25).

But the reform lasts only as long as Josiah's reign. As soon as he dies, yet another bad king takes his place, and the people lapse back into their old ways. So, in 586 BC, God gives Judah over to the Babylonians. The Babylonians kill the reigning Davidic king, destroy the temple, and deport the people into exile.

The Davidic Dynasty had lasted more than four hundred years, which is one of the longest unbroken dynasties in history. But four hundred years is not forever, and to the people of Judah, in 586, it seems as if God had gone back on his promise to David.

SELECTED READING:
Father Joseph L. Ponessa, Sharon Doran, Laurie Watson Manhardt, "Rehoboam," in *Come and See: The Rise and Fall of Israel*, pp. 85–86

For seventy-two years the family of Jesse ruled the twelve tribes all together—David for thirty-two years and Solomon for forty. Over the course of seven decades these two kings laid the firm foundations for the Israelite state. David faced many challenges to his authority, Solomon not so many. While all seemed well, tensions brewed beneath the surface. The crisis point came with the death of Solomon.

The succession process had little precedent to follow. Saul was killed in battle, his son was assassinated, David faced rebellions from his own sons during his lifetime, and only Solomon had a peaceful transition (even though he had his own half-brother Adonijah executed for trying to seize the throne). When Solomon dies, the continuity of the state depends upon the character of his heir. Had Israel known three great monarchs in a row, they might have become the equal of any power then on earth, but that was not meant to be.

Through prophecy, David knew that a son of his would always sit upon the throne, but how many other people were aware of this?

In their minds, many Israelites undoubtedly thought that the most capable person should rule, as in the days of the Judges. The son of Solomon met the test of prophecy, but he was not the most able man in the kingdom. One woman had the strength to set her son on the throne of Solomon, but he would not prove wise enough to keep the kingdom whole.

Queen Mother Naamah—Of Solomon's thousand wives and concubines, only one is known by name. Naamah, "The Agreeable One," was an Ammonite princess. The Ammonites and Moabites lived east of the Jordan and were distant relatives of the Hebrews with whom they had on-again, off-again relationships. Their historical position was one of belligerent neutrality—not really an enemy, but not an ally either. King David defeated them and absorbed their kingdoms, but behaved nobly toward them and won their friendship. The Ammonites gave one of their princesses to be a wife of Solomon, and she provided his child, who is mentioned in the Bible as the heir Rehoboam.

The Ammonites were descendants of Lot, the nephew of Abraham, but did not have an Abrahamic religion. They worshipped many deities, the gods of the children of Ammon (Judges 10:6), chief of which was Milcom (perhaps a variant of the Punic and Canaanite god Moloch), the abomination of the children of Ammon (1 Kings 11:7; 2 Kings 23:13). For Naamah, Solomon built a high place of Milcom on the Mount of Olives, across the Kidron Valley from the temple of the Lord on Mount Moriah. The God of Rehoboam's father dwelt in the big temple, and the god of Rehoboam's mother in the small one. Small wonder that the son ends up confused!

Accession of Rehoboam—Rehoboam takes the throne without any challenge from any half-brothers. This should have made the succession easy. The Hebrews petition him for relief from the forced labor they had endured under Solomon. They built a temple; they built a palace. Those jobs were finished. Why should conscription continue? Instead of wisely considering their plea, Rehoboam heeds his peers and threatens to multiply their work ten-fold. Such an approach had not worked for Pharaoh in Egypt, nor does it work for Rehoboam in Israel.

The Secession—The northern tribes withdraw support from Rehoboam's kingship, yet his own tribe of Judah remains loyal, along with the Levites who run the temple, and the desert tribe of Simeon. Did these not suffer under the levies also? Levi is certainly exempt as the priestly tribe, but perhaps the levies are not the only cause for this division of the land. Was slavery, for example, the only cause for the Civil War between the states? If so, why did the border-states, where slavery was legal, remain in the Union? History does not always succeed in unearthing the core issues of the time, but draws its own conclusions from later unfolding of events.

The tribe of Ephraim had always taken a leadership role in Hebrew affairs. Joseph, son of Jacob and Rachel and father of Ephraim, had saved the lives of all his family by becoming Prefect of Egypt. Joshua belonged to the tribe of Ephraim, and assigned his own populous tribe a large swath of territory in the midsection of the land. The wealthy Abdon judged Israel for eight years and was buried in his own land of Ephraim (Judges 12:13–15).

The Ephraimites let the little tribe of Benjamin (their full brother, son of Rachel and Jacob) have the first two kings, Saul and Ish-Bosheth. Then they let Judah (their three-quarter brother, son of Leah and Jacob) have the next two kings, David and Solomon. Now they honestly think it is their turn. They see how the son of Solomon is over-reaching and so they declare independence. They make two very big mistakes: 1) underestimating the dynastic strength of the House of David, and 2) overestimating the ability of the north to survive on its own.

The secession of the northern tribes in 922 BC[1] becomes the pivotal point in the history of Israel, when the trajectory passes from ascent to descent. Until then, Israel was on the rise; now Israel begins to fall. North and south could only be weaker separately than they had been together. The north may have had the advantage numer-

---

[1]   Or possibly 930 BC.

ically and economically, but the south held the advantage morally and theologically. Dividing their strengths and assets, they made it easier for their neighbors to pick them off one-by-one.

QUESTIONS FOR REVIEW

1. For what gift did Solomon ask God?
2. What did Solomon build?
3. Under Solomon, how did Israel's relationship with other nations change?
4. How did Solomon betray God?
5. What happened to the Kingdom of Israel under Solomon's son?

QUESTIONS FOR DISCUSSION

1. If God allowed you, like Solomon, to choose a gift that would help you serve him, what would you ask for? Why?
2. Why is wealth and power so tempting? Have you ever seen someone corrupted by them? Explain.
3. Why, after all God had done for them, do you think Israel chased after other gods? How are we all tempted in a similar way?

Chapter 3

LATER HISTORICAL BOOKS

Ezra and Nehemiah

||| ASSIGNED READING
||| Ezra 1, 4, 6, 8, 10
||| Nehemiah 1–2, 6, 8–9, 13

After the fall of Jerusalem, tens of thousands of Jews—the name given to those from the from the Southern Kingdom of Judah—are taken captive and forced to make their home in Babylon. There, they have no money, no influence, and no power. But they do have God. Stripped of all the worldly things they had once considered important, those Jews living in exile rediscover the faith of their ancestors. They begin studying the holy books and resurrecting ancient prayers and feasts.

In many ways, the Babylonian captivity is a time of great renewal for the Jewish people. At the same time, as the decades pass, they also grow comfortable in Babylon. They marry foreigners, start businesses, and build a community there. Because of this, when the Babylonian Empire falls to Cyrus the Great of Persia in 539 BC, and Cyrus grants them permission to return to Jerusalem, many choose not to take him up on his offer. They know no other home but Babylon, and don't want to leave it for a war-torn and ruined city like Jerusalem.

Those who do decide to return, though, have Cyrus' help. He even promises to help them rebuild their temple. The books of Ezra and Nehemiah (sometimes called 1 and 2 Esdras) begin with Cyrus' proclamation that the Jewish exiles in Babylon may return to their homeland. The books then recount what transpires as the Jews attempt to re-found their city. The task is not an easy one, even with Cyrus' help. Many of the neighboring peoples don't want the Jewish people in Jerusalem. Moreover, the Ark of the Covenant is gone, reportedly hidden in a cave by the prophet Jeremiah (2 Macc 2:5), so the few people who return have neither the money to restore the beauty of the temple nor the Ark to restore its spiritual importance.

Many years pass, and once again, the Jews living in Jerusalem begin committing the same sins as their ancestors. Finally, as the Book of Ezra tells us, the Persian King Artaxerxes sends Ezra, a priest and scribe, to Jerusalem to teach the people the law. When Ezra arrives, he immediately begins instructing people in the Scriptures, reading the law to people in the assembly, and persuading them to give up their foreign wives and ways. With Ezra's help, the Jewish refocus their lives on God, and, with the support of the Persian king, finally rededicate the Temple and celebrate the Passover feast.

The Book of Nehemiah begins with Nehemiah, cupbearer to King Artaxerxes, receiving a report that those who returned to Jerusalem from exile were in trouble and that Jerusalem's wall had been breached. After praying and fasting for his people, Nehemiah asks the king if he may go to Jerusalem to help the Jews (Neh 2:5). Artaxerxes not only grants permission, but names Nehemiah governor of Judah.

When Nehemiah arrives in Jerusalem, he discovers that surrounding rulers and nations (e.g., Arabs, Ammonites, Ashdodites) are trying to curtail the restoration of the city. Despite their attempts to thwart his efforts, Nehemiah rebuilds the walls around the city and, at his request, Ezra reads from the Book of the Law to all the people gathered. After hearing Ezra, the Jewish people cry out to God in sorrow for their sins. They fast, put on sackcloth (Neh 9:1), and make a covenant in which they promise not to disregard worship for the Lord or marry off their children to foreigners.

1 and 2 Maccabees

Just as the Babylonian Empire fell to the Persian Empire under Cyrus the Great in 539 BC, so the Persian Empire fell to the Macedonian Empire under Alexander the Great in 331 BC. Accordingly, Judea first becomes part of Alexander's great empire, and then, after his death, falls under the rule of the Greek king Antiochus Epiphanes.

Unlike Cyrus, Epiphanes has no interest in helping the Jewish people nor any tolerance for their religious practices. He wants them to worship the Greek gods, like everyone else in his empire, and so he erects a statue of Zeus in the Jerusalem temple. All the Jewish people, under pain of death, are ordered to offer sacrifices to the Greek gods. Many comply, adopting Greek religious and cultural practices in order to maintain or gain influence and wealth.

About 167 BC, though, a group of brothers, Judas (Maccabeus), Jonathan, and Simon, push back against their Greek rulers. Their revolt succeeds, and for the first time in several hundred years, Israel is an independent nation, ruled by no one but the Jews.

Eventually, the Maccabees rededicate the temple in 164 BC and hand on the rule of Judea to their descendants. They continue to rule as the Hasmonean Dynasty until the Romans conquer them in 63 BC. Importantly, though, even though it seemed in a way like the Kingdom of David had been restored, the Maccabees were not of the line of David. They had no claim by divine right to the throne. That belonged to someone still to come.

SELECTED READING:

St. Ambrose of Milan, *Three Books on the Duties of the Clergy*, I.XLI.1.209[1]

But as fortitude is proved not only by prosperity but also in adversity, let us now consider the death of Judas Maceabaeus. For he, after Nicanor, the general of King Demetrius, was defeated, boldly engaged 20,000 of the king's army with 900 men who were anxious to retire for fear of being overcome by so great a multitude, but whom he persuaded to endure a glorious death rather than to retire in disgraceful flight. "Let us not leave," he says, "any stain upon our glory." Thus, then, engaging in battle after having fought from sunrise until evening, he attacks and quickly drives back the right wing, where he sees the strongest troop of the enemy to be. But whilst pursuing the fugitives from the rear he gave a chance for a wound to be inflicted. Thus he found the spot of death more full of glory for himself than any triumph.

Why need I further mention his brother Jonathan, who fought against the king's force, with but a small troop. Though forsaken by his men, and left with only two, he retrieved the battle, drove back the enemy, and recalled his own men, who were flying in every direction, to share in his triumph.

Here then is fortitude in war, which bears no light impress of what is virtuous and seemly upon it, for it prefers death to slavery and disgrace. But what am I to say of the suffering of the martyrs? Not to go too far abroad, did the children of the Maccabaeus gain triumphs over the proud King Antiochus, as great as those of their fathers? The latter in truth were armed, but they conquered without arms. The company of the seven brothers stood unconquered, though surrounded by the legions of the king—tortures failed, tormentors ceased; but the martyrs failed not. One, having had the skin of his head pulled off, though changed in appearance, grew in

---

[1] Ambrose of Milan, *Sacred Writings of Saint Ambrose* (Bayern, DE: Jazzybee Verlag Jürgen Beck, 2017), 50.

courage. Another bidden to put forth his tongue, so that it might be cut off, answered, "The Lord hears not only those who speak, for He heard Moses when silent. He hears better the silent thoughts of His own than the voice of all others. Dost thou fear the scourge of my tongue—and dost thou not fear the scourge of blood spilt upon the ground? Blood, too, has a voice whereby it cries aloud to God—as it did in the case of Abel."

What shall I say of the mother who with joy looked on the corpse of her children as so many trophies and found delight in the voices of her dying sons, as though in the songs of singers, noting in her children the tones of the glorious harp of her own heart, and a sweeter harmony of love than any strain of the lute could give?

QUESTIONS FOR REVIEW

1. What happened to the faith of the Jews during their time in Babylon?
2. What great figure in Jewish history went to Jerusalem to help rebuild the temple after the Babylonian captivity ended?
3. What great figure in Jewish history went to Jerusalem to teach God's people the law?
4. Who was Antiochus Epiphanes, and what did he demand of the Jewish people?
5. Who were the Maccabees and what did they accomplish?

QUESTIONS FOR DISCUSSION

1. Why do you think the Jewish people viewed marrying people of other religions as dangerous? How important is it to you to marry someone of your own faith? Explain.
2. If you had been a Jew, living comfortably in Babylon under Cyrus, would you have wanted to return to Jerusalem? Why or why not?
3. For what or for whom would you give your life, as the seven brothers did? Explain.

The Chronology of the Old Testament[2]

Event	Date	Scriptural Reference
From Creation to the Exodus		
Primeval history	Dates Unknown	Gen 1–11
Abraham leaves Ur	c. 2090 BC	Gen 12:1–3
Jacob's Family Migrates to Egypt	c. 1876 BC	Gen 46:8–27
The Exodus	c. 1446 BC	Exod 12–13
Israel Conquers and Occupies Canaan		
The Wilderness Wanderings	c. 1446–1406 BC	Num 14:34–35; Deut 2:7
Beginning of the Conquest	c. 1406 BC	Josh 1–12
The Time of the Judges	c. 1350–1050 BC	Judg 1–1 Sam 9; cf. Judg 11:26
The United Monarchy		
The Kingship of Saul	1050–1010 BC	1 Sam 13:1; Acts 13:21
The Kingship of David	1010–970 BC	2 Sam 5:3–5
The Kingship of Solomon	970–930 BC	1 Kgs 11:42
Work on the Temple Begins	966 BC	1 Kgs 6:1
The Divided Monarchy		
The Kingdom Divides	930 BC	1 Kgs 12
Assyrian Conquest of Israel	722 BC	2 Kgs 17
Babylonian Conquest of Judah	586 BC	2 Kgs 24–25
Return from Exile and Restoration		
Babylonian Captivity Ends	538 BC	Ezra 1
Reconstruction of Jerusalem Temple	520–515 BC	Ezra 6:14–15
Reconstruction of Jerusalem Walls	445 BC	Neh 1–6
The Maccabean Period		
Antiochus Epiphanes IV Outlaws Judaism	167 BC	1 Mac 1:20–64
Judas Maccabeus Rededicates Temple	164 BC	1 Mac 4:36–61
Romans Seize Control of Palestine	63 BC	———

---

[2] Ignatius Catholic Study Bible, "Old Testament Chronology," 1 Samuel 14.

PART IV

THE BOOKS OF WISDOM AND PROPHECY

The Old Covenant and the New Covenant are like two sides of a coin: they are distinct, but one. Each belongs to God's plan for our salvation, and although they can seem radically different at first glance, closer examination shows us how interconnected they are. We've already seen many of those connections in our study of typology. The Old Covenant is filled with people, places, events, and things that point forward to the New Covenant, illuminating Jesus Christ and his mission.

The Books of Wisdom and Prophecy also connect the Old and New Covenants, although they do this in a somewhat different way. In effect, they form a bridge between the Old Covenant and the New Covenant.

The Books of Wisdom (or wisdom literature) do this as the literary expression of the Davidic Covenant. Although not all of them were written during the reign of David and Solomon, some were. Moreover, the books reflect Israel's mission, which flowered under David and Solomon, to lead other nations to God. They both draw on the literary traditions of other nations—something made possible by the extent to which the Israelites interacted freely with their neighbors during the height of the nation's power—and were intended for the moral and religious instruction of other nations. The wisdom they contain is universal—helpful for all people in all times and not specific to one nation. In this sense, the Wisdom Books point forward to the New Covenant and the Gospel message, which also was not only for the Jews and the descendants of Moses, but for all people, in all times.

The prophets are a bit different. These men and women were called by God to proclaim truth to the Israelites. Sometimes the truth they proclaimed was repentance; they called people to give up their sinful ways and come back to the God who loved them. Other times, the truth they proclaimed was a warning; they predicted harsh punishments being visited upon the people if they did not repent. Prophets also talked about God's love, his mission for Israel, and his faithfulness in the face of their sin.

Above all, the prophets proclaimed a coming Messiah and a New Covenant. In the darkest moments of the Israelites' history—moments of war, destruction, and exile—the prophets gave people hope. They assured the Israelites that God had not forgotten his people. There would be a Savior, and God would gather his people into one family once more. In later years, both Jesus and the Apostles would point back to the prophets, showing how their words were fulfilled in Christ and the Church.

Let's look now at these bridges, starting with the Books of Wisdom.

Chapter 1

The Books of Wisdom

Job and the Problem of Suffering

|| Assigned Reading
|| Job 1–3, 27, 29, 32, 38, 40, 42

Why do we suffer? Why does a good God allow suffering? And how are
we to respond?

These are the questions addressed by the Book of Job. The story
centers on the plight of Job, a just and well-to-do man who suddenly loses
everything he had: his children, his wealth, his servants, and his health.
As Job sits with his wife, mourning their losses, three old friends come to
visit him. In an attempt to be helpful, the friends offer various answers to
the problem of suffering. Primarily, they believe that Job's suffering must
be his fault; they see it as a punishment for his sins.

Job's wife, on the other hand, wants her suffering husband to "curse
God, and die" (Job 2:9). Job calls her advice foolish, and yet he knows
has done nothing to merit the degree of suffering inflicted upon him. At
this point, God speaks to him. He reminds Job of his wisdom and power,
of all the mysteries on heaven and earth that Job can't understand, and
of man's littleness in the sweep of the universe. Job, in response, bows

before the mystery of suffering, choosing to trust God rather than curse him. God, in return, blesses Job abundantly, returning to him all that he had lost and more.

The Psalms: The Prayer of God's People

|| ASSIGNED READING
|| Psalms 1, 22–23, 42, 51, 89, 110, 136, 150

The Book of Psalms is a collection of hymns written for the liturgical worship of the Israelites and still used in the worship of the Church. Some psalms are laments, others are songs of victory or joyful celebration, while still others are deep and heart-wrenching pleas for forgiveness.

According to tradition, David authored many of the psalms, and Scripture is consistent this claim. His name is attached to seventy-three of the one hundred-fifty psalms; 2 Samuel refers him as "the sweet psalmist of Israel" (2 Sam 23:1); and elsewhere David is depicted singing to and producing music for God. Even if David didn't compose all the psalms attributed to him, though, scholars still believe he may have sponsored some of them, or they were written in tribute to him. Regardless, other human authors did have some hand in writing the psalms, and Asaph, Heman, Ethan, Moses, and others are all accredited for composing some of them.

The Psalter, which is what we often call the Book of Psalms, was a book written on the heart of Israel. People knew many of the psalms by heart and quoted them often. So, in Scripture, we see Jesus reciting Psalm 22 on the cross and the devil using Psalm 91 when he tempts Jesus to sin (Luke 4:9–11). The same holds true today. With the psalms recited or sung at every Holy Mass and incorporated into the Liturgy of the Hours, the psalms remain one of the most important prayers of the Church. Many people also turn to the psalms for their private prayer, identifying with the rich range of emotions they express. Whatever you're feeling—

grief, frustration, sorrow, love, gratitude, anger, loneliness, confusion, betrayal—there is a psalm that expresses that emotion and can help you turn that feeling into a prayer.

Proverbs, Ecclesiastes, Song of Songs, Wisdom, Sirach

ASSIGNED READING
Proverbs 3, 8, 24, 31
Ecclesiastes 1, 3, 12
Song of Solomon 1
Wisdom of Solomon 3, 7–9, 13, 24
Sirach prologue, 1, 3, 6, 30

Proverbs is a collection of wisdom sayings, many of which are attributed to King Solomon. Some of these sayings are practical, offering pithy advice for daily living and growing in human maturity. Others seek to illuminate the nature of wisdom. One in particular, cited as "the words of Lemuel, king of Massa, which his mother taught him," focuses on what qualities a man should look for in a wife (see Prov 31).

The purpose of Proverbs is summed up in the first few verses of the book:

That men may know wisdom and instruction,
    understand words of insight,
receive instruction in wise dealing,
    righteousness, justice, and equity;
that prudence may be given to the simple,
    knowledge and discretion to the youth—
the wise man also may hear and increase in learning,
    and the man of understanding acquire skill,
to understand a proverb and a figure,

the words of the wise and their riddles.
The fear of the LORD is the beginning of knowledge;
    fools despise wisdom and instruction. (Prov 1:2–7)

The Book of Ecclesiastes, also known as Qoheleth, or "one who brings together an assembly," is also traditionally attributed to Solomon, although it may have been written by another king in the Davidic lineage or someone else writing in the tradition of Solomon. This book treats some of the deepest questions of life, specifically vanity and the passing nature of the world. In a sense, it is the Bible's only book of philosophy, reflecting man's search for meaning.

The next Wisdom Book, the Song of Songs (meaning the ultimate or best song), is also known as the Song of Solomon or Canticle of Canticles. It is a love song, sung by a lover to his beloved. Like much of Scripture, the song contains layers of meaning. On one level, it can be read as a beautiful expression of human love and the glories of marriage. It also can be read as a love song from God to Israel, which points forward to the love between Christ and his Church. And it can be read as a love song from Jesus to each one of us; it hints at the desire God has for each and every soul:

Set me as a seal upon your heart,
    as a seal upon your arm;
for love is strong as death,
    jealousy is cruel as the grave.
Its flashes are flashes of fire,
    a most vehement flame.
Many waters cannot quench love,
    neither can floods drown it. (Song 8:6–7)

The Book of Wisdom, which is also called the Wisdom of Solomon, was probably written a century or less before the birth of Jesus. It looks first at the virtue of justice (Wis 1–6), then wisdom (Wis 6–11), and then the Exodus (Wis 11–19), giving praise to God throughout.

Last, the Book of Sirach, also known as Ecclesiasticus, is the last book to be written in the Old Testament, during the first century BC. It was originally written in Hebrew by "Jesus the son of Sirach, son of Eleazar" (Sir 50:27) but was translated into Greek by the author's grandson (as indicated in the prologue to the book). The author begins by writing about wisdom, and then gives us poetic advice about different aspects of life, such as raising children, staying healthy, and how to relate to God and other people. It ends by giving homage to some of the greatest figures of the Old Testament (Sir 44–50).

SELECTED READING:
Pope St. Gregory the Great, *Commentary on the Song of Songs*, nos. 1–4

When the human race was banished from the joys of paradise, it embarked upon the pilgrimage of this present life with a heart blind to spiritual understanding. If the divine voice were to proclaim to this blind heart, "Follow God!" or "Love God!"—as it was proclaimed to it in the Law—once it was uttered, the frigid sluggishness of spiritual insensitivity would have prevented it from grasping what it heard. And so, a divine discourse is communicated to the frigid, sluggish soul by means of enigmas and secretly teaches such a soul the love that it does not know by means of what it knows.

Allegory functions as a device to lift the soul that is far from God to God. This is possible because allegories employ enigmas. When the soul recognizes something familiar to itself in the words of an enigma, it comes to understand in the deeper meaning of the enigma's words what is not familiar to itself and is thereby separated from the earth by means of earthly terminology. By approaching what it already knows, the soul comes to understand what is unknown to it. To create allegories, the divine thoughts are cloaked with what we know; by examining exterior language, we attain an interior understanding.

For this reason the Song of Songs employs language characteristic of sensual love to reheat the soul using familiar expressions to revive it from sluggishness and to spur it onto the love that is above using language typical of the love here below. This book mentions kisses and breasts and cheeks and thighs. We must not ridicule the sacred description of these terms but reflect upon the mercy of God. For this book goes so far as to extend the meaning of the language characteristic of our shameful love in such a way that our heart is set on fire with yearning for that sacred love. By discussing the parts of the body, this book summons us to love. Therefore we ought to note how wonderfully and mercifully this book is working within us. However, from where God lowers himself by speaking, he lifts us up there by understanding. We are instructed by the conversations proper to sensual love when their power causes us to enthusiastically burn with love for the Divinity.

Moreover, we ought to consider this book shrewdly lest we become stuck on exterior perceptions when we hear the language of exterior love and the very device employed to lift us up instead weighs us down and fails to lift us up. In this exterior, sensual language we must seek whatever is interior and discuss the body as if we were apart from the body. We ought to come to this sacred wedding of the bride and bridegroom clothed in wedding garments, that is, able to understand profound charity. Such attire is necessary lest, not dressed in wedding garments, that is, not having an understanding that is worthy of comprehending charity, we are banished from this wedding banquet into the exterior darkness, that is, into the blindness of ignorance.

We must transcend this language that is typical of the passions so as to realize that virtuous state in which we are unable to be influenced by the passions. As the sacred writings employ words and meanings, so a picture employs colors and subject matter; it is excessively foolish to cling to the colors of the picture in such a way that the subject painted is ignored. Now if we embrace the words that are expressed in exterior terms and ignore their deeper meanings, it is like ignoring the subject depicted while focusing upon the colors alone. It is written that the letter kills but that the spirit gives life. As the letter cloaks the spirit, so a husk veils corn. But feeding on the husk is the lot of beasts of burden; human beings feed on corn. The one who uses his human reason shucks a spiritual ear of corn, casting away the husks of the beasts of burden and hastening to eat the corn. For the sake of this endeavor it is surely useful to veil the mysteries with the wrapping of letters, for long-sought wisdom tastes better.

For this reason it is written, "The wise conceal understanding" (Prov 10:14), for spiritual understanding is without a doubt cloaked under the veil of the letter. For this reason again, it is said in the same book, "It is the glory of God to hide the word" (Prov 25:2). Since the glorious God reveals himself to the mind seeking God, he ought all the more be craftily searched for interiorly that he may reveal himself. But should we be demanding what God hides in his mysteries? Of course we should, for it follows, "And the glory of kings is to search into the word" (Prov 25:2). They are kings who already know how to rule their bodies and how to search into the stirrings of their flesh. And so, the glory of kings is to search into the word; praise [is given to] those who live a good life because they thoroughly scrutinize the secrets of God's commandments.

QUESTIONS FOR REVIEW

1. With which problem of human existence does the Book of Job wrestle?
2. What biblical figure is the main contributor to the Psalms?
3. What are the three primary ways we can read and interpret the Song of Solomon?
4. Which book of biblical wisdom literature wrestles with the problem of vanity?
5. What was the last book of the Old Testament that was written? When was it written?

QUESTIONS FOR DISCUSSION

1. What are some of the problems or anxieties with which you're currently wrestling? Do you believe the Bible has something to say to those problems? Why or why not?
2. Do you find it strange that God would use the love between a man and a woman as an allegory for the love he feels for us? Why or why not?
3. Of all the assigned biblical readings for this chapter, what piece of advice that you read in the wisdom literature has stuck with you the most? How does this apply to your life right now?

Chapter 2

The Books of the Prophets

The prophets interpreted signs of the times in light of the covenant. As people called by God to speak to his people, they suffered and sacrificed to bring the Israelites back to a right relationship with him. Accordingly, the prophetic books span hundreds of years of Israel's history, from before the fall of the Northern Kingdom to after the return of the Jewish people to Jerusalem.

In the Bible, there are four major prophets and twelve minor prophets, for a total of sixteen. It's important, though, to note that the terms "major" and "minor" don't necessarily imply that one prophet was more or less important than another, only that some prophetic books are longer than others.

Isaiah

ASSIGNED READING
Isaiah 7, 9, 10, 11, 42, 49, 55

In the eighth century BC, before the fall of the Northern Kingdom, a man named Isaiah was called by God to urge the people of Israel and Judah to change their ways and return to the Lord or face the destruction of their kingdoms. Although the Book of Isaiah is full of words of warning for a wayward people, it is most well known for its words of hope. Those words focus on the holiness of God and the promised Messiah, who will suffer in the people's stead.

Long before Jesus' birth, Isaiah told the people that the Messiah would be born of a virgin and reign over an everlasting kingdom (Isa 7:14; 9:6–7). He also foresaw the gifts of the Holy Spirit—gifts bestowed on each of us in the Sacrament of Confirmation: wisdom, understanding, counsel, might, knowledge, and fear of the Lord (Isa 11:2). Likewise, after the fall of the Northern Kingdom to the Assyrians, Isaiah spoke of a servant who would "bring Jacob back to him" so "that Israel might be gathered to him" and "restore the preserved of Israel" (49:5–6). This servant would be "a light to the nations," making it possible for God's salvation to "reach to the end of the earth" (Isa 49:6).

When Jesus finally came, many people struggled to see that he was the promised Messiah, because he wasn't a great and powerful political ruler. Jesus didn't attempt to restore (or even seem interested in restoring) the earthly Kingdom of David. He organized no armies. He led no revolts. The people of his day were so focused on Isaiah's words about an everlasting kingdom that they missed much of what Isaiah had to say about the Messiah's suffering. Yet, Isaiah predicted in great detail all that Jesus would have to suffer on Good Friday.

Speaking in the voice of that future Messiah, Isaiah writes, "I gave my back to those who struck me, and my cheeks to those who pulled out the beard; I hid not my face from shame and spitting" (Isa 50:6). He also describes the Messiah as one "despised and rejected by men; a man of sorrows, and acquainted with grief" (53:3). Then, in one of the longest "Suffering Servant" passages, Isaiah tells us why the Messiah will have to suffer so.

> Surely he has borne our griefs
>   and carried our sorrows;
> yet we esteemed him stricken,
>   struck down by God, and afflicted.
> But he was wounded for our transgressions,

he was bruised for our iniquities;
    upon him was the chastisement that made us whole,
        and with his stripes we are healed.
All we like sheep have gone astray;
        we have turned every one to his own way;
and the LORD has laid on him
        the iniquity of us all. (Isa 53:4–6)

"Like a lamb that is led to the slaughter," the Suffering Servant is innocent. He has done no wrong. Yet he humbly submits to the judgment of his oppressors, for the sake of his people (Isa 53:7–9).

Isaiah's words are repeatedly quoted in the New Testament. They are, in fact, quoted more than those of any other prophet. But in Isaiah's times, the people refused to listen to him. Israel fell in Isaiah's lifetime, and before he died, he warned that Judah would be next.

Jeremiah

|| ASSIGNED READING
|| Jeremiah 1, 30–33

After Isaiah's death, God tasked another man, this one from a family of priests, with calling the people to repentance. This man, Jeremiah, was a reluctant prophet. He knew the people wouldn't listen to him. He knew he would be despised and rejected for what he would say to them. He was also a young man—perhaps in his teens—when God first called him. He tried to use that as an excuse not to do as God asked, but God rebuked Jeremiah for that, saying, "Do not say, 'I am only a youth'; for to all to whom I send you you shall go, and whatever I command you you shall speak. Be not afraid of them, for I am with you to deliver you" (Jer 1:7–8).

Like Isaiah before him, Jeremiah warned the people of Judah that if they did not change their ways, God would give them over to their enemies and they would be exiled from their land. He then watched what happened when that warning was not heeded, witnessing the destruction of Jerusalem at the hand of the Babylonians.

Also like Isaiah, though, Jeremiah told the people that exile would not be the end. Despite the fact that the ten Northern Tribes had long since disappeared among the nations, Jeremiah prophesied that the Lord would bring them back to Israel, along with all those from the Southern Kingdom taken by the Babylonians, and restore the Kingdom of David:

> And it shall come to pass in that day, says the LORD of hosts, that I will break the yoke from off their neck, and I will burst their bonds, and strangers shall no more make servants of them. But they shall serve the LORD their God and David their king, whom I will raise up for them.

> Then fear not, O Jacob my servant, says the LORD,
>   nor be dismayed, O Israel;
> for behold, I will save you from afar,
> and your offspring from the land of their captivity.
> Jacob shall return and have quiet and ease,
> and none shall make him afraid. (Jer 30:8–10)

In one of the most important passages from Jeremiah, the prophet foresees a "new covenant," one in which the law is no longer written on tablets of stone, but rather on the hearts of men. In other words, Jeremiah sees a time coming when people will obey the Lord as they were always meant to obey him—out of love:

> Behold, the days are coming, says the LORD, when I will make a new covenant with the house of Israel and the house of Judah, not like the covenant which I made with their fathers when I took them by the hand to bring them out of the land of Egypt, my covenant which they broke, and I showed myself their Master, says the LORD. But this is the covenant which I will make with the house of Israel after those days, says the LORD: I will put my

law within them, and I will write it upon their hearts; and I will be their God, and they shall be my people. (Jer 31:31–33)

Ezekiel

|| ASSIGNED READING
|| Ezekiel 11, 18, 34–37, 40–43

God, like a loving father, let the Israelites suffer the consequences of their sins, but he never turned his back on them. Even as they lived in exile, he sent prophets to them to proclaim a message of hope and to help them walk in his ways. Ezekiel was one of those prophets. Born into a priestly family and exiled at a young age, he spent most of his life in Babylon. There, he helped bring about the religious renewal that took place among the Jewish people. He gathered people together to pray (anticipating the synagogues that would flourish in Jesus' day), spoke about the coming New Covenant, and called people not just to worship God, but to love him.

In particular, Ezekiel focused on softening the hearts of the Jewish people, so that God could "write" his law there, rather than on tablets of stone.

> Therefore say, "Thus says the Lord GOD: I will gather you from the peoples, and assemble you out of the countries where you have been scattered, and I will give you the land of Israel." And when they come there, they will remove from it all its detestable things and all its abominations. And I will give them one heart, and put a new spirit within them; I will take the stony heart out of their flesh and give them a heart of flesh, that they may walk in my statutes and keep my ordinances and obey them; and they shall be my people, and I will be their God. (Ezek 11:17–20)

Like the prophets that came before him, Ezekiel sees God gathering his people out of all the nations. He also anticipates the New Testament writers, describing the people as sheep and God as their shepherd (Ezek 34), and having a vision of a new temple (Ezek 40–43), much like that later seen in the Book of Revelation, in which God will reside, dwelling in his people's midst: "My dwelling place shall be with them; and I will be their God, and they shall be my people. Then the nations will know that I the LORD sanctify Israel, when my sanctuary is in the midst of them for evermore" (Ezek 37:27–28).

Daniel

|| ASSIGNED READING
|| Daniel 1, 2, 7, 9, 11

Daniel is another prophet who lived in exile. Written in three different languages (Aramaic, Greek, and Hebrew), the events of the Book of Daniel unfold in the sixth century, during the reigns of both King Nebuchadnezzar and Cyrus of Persia. Unlike the other prophets, the Book of Daniel contains longer narrative accounts and is sometimes classified as apocalyptic literature for its visions of international conflict and great trouble.

Daniel, similar to the patriarch Joseph, becomes a favorite of King Nebuchadnezzar due to his ability to interpret dreams. Daniel himself ends up experiencing many visions of kingdoms that would rule and then collapse leading up to the coming of the Messiah after "Seventy weeks of years" (Dan 9:24). His visions of conflict also include visions of what comes after the conflict, such as people rising from the dead, "some to everlasting life, and some to shame and everlasting contempt" (Dan 12:2).

Daniel also foresaw "the saints of the Most High," who would "receive the kingdom, and possess the kingdom for ever, for ever and ever" (Dan 7:18) and one who came "like a son of man":

I saw in the night visions,
and behold, with the clouds of heaven
    there came one like a son of man,
and he came to the Ancient of Days
    and was presented before him.
And to him was given dominion
    and glory and kingdom,
that all peoples, nations, and languages
    should serve him;
his dominion is an everlasting dominion,
    which shall not pass away,
and his kingdom one
    that shall not be destroyed. (Dan 7:13–14)

The Minor Prophets

The shorter prophetic books, referred to as the minor prophets, span several hundred years, from Amos and Hosea (eighth century BC) to Malachi and Joel (fifth to fourth century BC). Like Isaiah, Jeremiah, Ezekiel, and Daniel, they proclaim a message of repentance and hope, urging people to faithfulness now and promising a time of healing and peace in the future. The twelve minor prophets are:

- **Hosea:** During the eighth century, Hosea preached against the rampant idolatry of his time, comparing Israel to an adulterous wife and God to the faithful husband who waits for her return and restores her to a place of honor.
- **Joel:** A post-exilic prophet who envisioned the Spirit of God pouring out on the covenant people. What he saw was the messianic age, inaugurated at the first Christian Pentecost, when the Holy Spirit came mightily upon the Church.
- **Amos:** Before the fall of the Northern Kingdom, Amos, a shepherd of Judah, warned of its coming destruction and condemned those who lived in wealth and luxury while ignoring the less fortunate.

- **Obadiah:** Although scholars remain uncertain about the century in which Obadiah lived, his prophecies are directed at the people of Edom, who were enemies of Judah both during and after the Babylonian exile, warning them against celebrating the destruction of Jerusalem.

- **Jonah:** Although it is believed that Jonah was truly a well-known prophet who lived in the eighth century BC, the Book of Jonah may have been written much later. Filled with dramatic events—such as Jonah spending three days in the belly of the whale—it illustrates that God will extend his mercy to anyone who seeks it.

- **Micah:** A contemporary of Isaiah, Micah strove to help the people of Judah understand that burnt offerings and sacrifices were not what God ultimately wanted from his people. Rather, he wanted them "to do justice, and to love kindness, and to walk humbly" with God (Mic 6:8).

- **Nahum:** In the early seventh century, after the fall of the Northern Kingdom, Nahum prophesied that Judah's great oppressor and enemy, Assyria, would soon be destroyed. Assyria was, in fact, destroyed in 612 BC.

- **Habakkuk:** A prophet of Judah before the fall of the Southern Kingdom, Habakkuk wasn't afraid to put tough questions to God. His book of prophecy is largely a dialogue with God. It wrestles with the question of how God can use a nation that is more wicked than Israel (the Babylonians) to punish the sins of Israel (the Southern Kingdom of Judah).

- **Zephaniah:** Written shortly before the religious reforms of King Josiah of Judah in the 620s BC, this mid-seventh-century prophet painted a dark picture of what was in store for Judah and all the nations who refused to acknowledge the sovereignty of God and walk in his ways.

- **Haggai:** Written after the exile to Babylon, Haggai's focus isn't on judgment for sins, but rather on exhortation to rebuild what was lost in the past, particularly the temple. Haggai assures the people that the temple will be filled with the Spirit of the Lord and will be greater than the temple of Solomon, despite its humble appearance (Hag 2:9).

- **Zechariah:** A contemporary of Haggai, Zechariah echoed Haggai's instructions to rebuild the temple, but focused more on the program for national restoration and the coming Messianic age.
- **Malachi:** Written most likely after the return of the Jewish people to Jerusalem, during the period of Ezra and Nehemiah, Malachi proclaims God's faithful love for his people, condemns the wrong practices of his people (from unclean sacrifices, to divorce, to marriage with Gentiles), and speaks of a pure sacrifice that will offered throughout the world in messianic times.

Throughout all the prophets, there is an increasing intensity to their expectation of a coming Messiah. Israel had staked its hope on a new covenant, in which all that they had lost would be restored, and in which God would honor his covenant with David, making Israel an everlasting kingdom, ruled forever by a Son of David.

That New Covenant would come. And God would honor his covenant with David. Only, the way in which it came and the way in which God did that wasn't exactly what the Jewish people were expecting.

SELECTED READING:
Pope Francis, Address to the German Altar Servers, August 4, 2015

I thank you all for coming in such great numbers, defying the heat of the Roman sun in August. I thank Bishop Nemet, your President, for his words of introduction and greeting. You have come from a variety of countries on a pilgrimage to Rome, the city where the Apostles Peter and Paul were martyred. It is important to realize that being close to Jesus and knowing him in the Eucharist through your service at the altar, enables you to open yourselves to others, to journey together, to set demanding goals and to find the strength to achieve them. It is a source of real joy to recognize that we are small and weak, all the while knowing that, with Jesus' help, we can be strengthened and take up the challenge of life's great journey in his company.

The prophet Isaiah also discovered this truth, which is to say that God purified his intentions, forgave his sins, healed his heart and made him ready to take up the important task of bringing God's word to his people. In so doing, he became an instrument of the presence of divine mercy. Isaiah found that, by entrusting himself to the hands of the Lord, his whole existence was transformed.

The biblical verse we have just heard speaks to us precisely of this. Isaiah has a vision through which he perceives the glory of the Lord, but at the same time, it shows that, although the Lord reveals himself, he still remains far off. Isaiah is astonished to discover that it is God who makes the first move—do not forget this: it is always God who makes the first move in our life—to discover, that it is God who approaches him first. Isaiah notices that divine action was not hindered by his imperfections; it was God's goodness alone that enabled him to take up the mission, transforming him into a totally new person and therefore one able to respond to the call of the Lord, saying, "Here am I! Send me" (Is 6:8).

You are more fortunate today than the prophet Isaiah. In the Eucharist and in the other sacraments, you experience the intimate closeness of Jesus, the sweetness and power of his presence. You do not meet Jesus sitting on an inaccessibly high throne, but in the Bread and Wine of the Eucharist. His word does not shake the doorposts, but rather caresses the strings of the heart. Like Isaiah, each of you sees that God, although making himself close to us in Jesus and bending lovingly down to you, always remains immeasurably greater, beyond our ability to understand him in his deepest being. Like Isaiah, you, too, have experienced that it is always God who takes the initiative, because it is he who created you and willed you into being. It is he who, in your baptism, has made you into a new creation; he is always patiently waiting for your response to his initiative, offering forgiveness to whoever asks him with humility.

If we do not resist him, Jesus will touch our lips with the flame of his merciful love, as he did the prophet Isaiah. This will make us worthy to receive him and to take him to our brothers and sisters. Like Isaiah, we, too, are invited not to stay closed within ourselves, protecting our faith in a cellar to which we withdraw in difficult moments. Rather, we are called to share the joy of knowing we are chosen and saved by God's mercy, the joy of being witnesses to the fact that faith gives new direction to our steps, that it makes us free and strong so as to be ready and prepared for the mission.

How beautiful it is to discover that faith brings us out of ourselves, out of our isolation. Precisely because we are filled with the joy of being friends with Jesus Christ, faith draws us towards others, making us natural missionaries!

QUESTIONS FOR REVIEW

1. How did the prophets connect the Old and New Testaments?
2. What is the difference between the major and minor prophets?
3. Who are the four major prophets?
4. Name four details revealed by those prophets about Christ and the New Covenant.
5. Name five of the twelve minor prophets.

QUESTIONS FOR DISCUSSION

1. What kind of greatness do the Suffering Servant passages in Isaiah depict? How is this different from the world's ideas of greatness?
2. Although few listened to the words they proclaimed, the prophets proclaimed them anyway. What does this tell us about being faithful to God's call?
3. Jeremiah tried to use his youth as a reason to not answer God's call. Do you ever do the same? If so, how? If not, why not?

Part V

The New Testament

Usually translations are a good thing. They make clear what was incomprehensible to us before. But even the best translations have their problems, and occasionally translators can select words that obscure rather than clarify. This, in a certain way, is the case with the use of the word "testament."

Hundreds and hundreds of years ago, when the Bible was being translated from Greek and Hebrew into Latin, the Latin translator took the Hebrew word for "covenant," *bĕrît* (in Greek *diathēkē*), and translated it as "testament." That has caused some problems because not only does the word "testament" not fully convey the meaning of a covenant, but dividing the canon into the Old and New Testaments obscures the fact that Scripture is really divided by covenants. It is the story of the Old Covenant and the New Covenant.

In the New Covenant, that story is told in twenty-seven books. Four of those books are the Gospels of Matthew, Mark, Luke, and John. These Gospels tell the story of Jesus' earthly life and ministry and were written either by Apostles (Matthew and John) or companions of the Apostles (Mark was a companion to Peter; Luke was a companion to Paul). The Book of Acts presents the history of the early Church and was also written by Luke. After that come the Epistles, which are letters to early Christian communities from Paul, Peter, James, Jude, and John. The last book of the Bible is the Book of Revelation, which recounts a vision of heaven and the end times that St. John the Apostle received on the island of Patmos.

All the books of the New Testament were written during the first century AD. While scholars differ on exactly when in the first century each was written, the majority were composed within a few decades after Jesus' death. That is to say, all the books were written and circulated during a time when countless people who had witnessed the events that the books recount still lived. The books were received into communities filled with people who either had known Jesus or had known people who knew Jesus. They weren't records of things that took place long ago, but records of things that took place within living memory of their authors and readers.

Chapter 1

An Introduction to the Gospels

When many of us hear the word "gospel," we think of the books of Matthew, Mark, Luke, and John. But the Gospel is much more than a book. The word itself actually means "good news" (it's the English translation of the Latin word *evangelium*), and that's what the Gospel is. It's the Good News of our salvation. It's the entirety of God's saving message for us: that he loves us so much that he became man, died on a cross, and rose again so that we could have eternal life. The Church is also part of that Good News. When Jesus ascended to heaven, he didn't leave us on our own to just figure things out as best as we could. He sent the Holy Spirit to guide a Church who could teach and interpret the Scriptures authoritatively and administer sacraments that were truly efficacious— sacraments that truly did what they signified.

Because of this, we call Matthew, Mark, Luke, and John's books about the life and death of Jesus "Gospels." If you had to sum up the Gospel in one word, though, it would simply be *Jesus*. Jesus is the Gospel. Jesus is the Good News. So, it makes sense that the books that tell us who he was, how he lived, what he taught, and what he did are specifically known as *the* Gospels.

The Composition of the Gospels

Although the Gospels are the first four books of the New Testament, they were written after, not before, many of the other books of the New Testament. It is because of what they contain that they are placed first. They give us the foundation for understanding the rest of the New Testament and show us how Jesus' life, teaching, and death all fulfill the promises God made in the Old Covenant and establish a New Covenant.

As we saw in the section on the canon, there were three stages in the formation of the Gospels. The first stage was the life and teaching of Jesus; Jesus was both the bearer of the Good News and the Good News himself. After Jesus' death and Resurrection, the Apostles, enlightened by the Holy Spirit, continued proclaiming that Good News in Judea, throughout the Roman Empire, and beyond. This second stage in the formation of the Gospels is called the oral tradition. Finally, the third and final stage arrived. This was the written Gospels. As the Catechism explains:

> The sacred authors, in writing the four Gospels, selected certain of the many elements which had been handed on, either orally or already in written form; others they synthesized or explained with an eye to the situation of the churches, the while sustaining the form of preaching, but always in such a fashion that they have told us the honest truth about Jesus [DV 19]. (CCC 126)

Among the four canonical Gospels, Matthew, Mark, and Luke are the most similar. Together, they are known as the Synoptic Gospels. The word "synoptic" comes from the same Greek word as "synopsis." Today, when we use synopsis, we typically mean "summary," but it also means "view together," which is how it's used in relation to the Gospels. These three can be "viewed together" because they have much in common.

The Gospel of John, on the other hand, differs in content and approach from the Synoptic Gospels. The reason for this may have something to do with it being (most likely) the last Gospel to be written. Since John would have seen the other Gospels, he may have felt it less necessary to include details in his Gospel that were already in Matthew, Mark, and Luke. Also, as the "beloved disciple" (John 19:27) who Tradition confirms took Mary into his home after Jesus' crucifixion, John would have had unique insights into Jesus' life and work that the other Apostles would not have possessed.

These differences are starkly clear at many points in the Gospels, including the events of the Last Supper. John had already presented a deep and developed theology of the Eucharist in John 6, which allowed him to write about other events that happened on the last night of Jesus' earthly life. You can see the differences in all four accounts below.

The Words of Institution in the Gospels*

Matthew 26:26–29	Now as they were eating, Jesus took bread, and blessed, and broke it, and gave it to the disciples and said, "**Take, eat; this is my body.**" And he took a chalice, and when he had given thanks he gave it to them, saying, "**Drink of it, all of you; for this is my blood of the covenant, which is poured out for many for the forgiveness of sins.** I tell you I shall not drink again of this fruit of the vine until that day when I drink it new with you in my Father's kingdom."
Mark 14:22–25	And as they were eating, he took bread, and blessed, and broke it, and gave it to them, and said, "**Take; this is my body.**" And he took a chalice, and when he had given thanks he gave it to them, and they all drank of it. And he said to them, "**This is my blood of the covenant, which is poured out for many.** Truly, I say to you, I shall not drink again of the fruit of the vine until that day when I drink it new in the kingdom of God."

*There is also an account in 1 Corinthians 11:23–26

Luke 22:14–20	And when the hour came, he sat at table, and the apostles with him. And he said to them, "I have earnestly desired to eat this Passover with you before I suffer; for I tell you I shall not eat it until it is fulfilled in the kingdom of God." And he took a chalice, and when he had given thanks he said, "**Take this**, and divide it among yourselves; for I tell you that from now on I shall not drink of the fruit of the vine until the kingdom of God comes." And he took bread, and when he had given thanks he broke it and gave it to them, saying, "**This is my body which is given for you.** Do this in remembrance of me." And likewise the chalice after supper, saying, "**This chalice which is poured out for you is the new covenant in my blood.**"
John 6	Not included in this Gospel, but John writes of the theology of the Eucharist in chapter 6

Although all four accounts contain minor differences, this has never been an issue for the Church. If you and three of your classmates were all asked to write down what happened at a party you went to together, your accounts would have some similarities and some differences. You might have witnessed the same things but done so from a different angle or with a different perspective on what was happening. Likewise, the more time you had to reflect on the party, the more likely your account of it would emphasize different points, based on what you found important. Either way, the differences wouldn't make your account any less true or important than your friends.' The same holds true for the Gospels. God, working through human authors, inspired all those authors to shine a unique light on the life and teaching of Jesus, enabling us to see a much more complete picture of the Gospel than if we only had one account.

The "Other Gospels"

There are, however, ancient accounts of Jesus' life that the Church does not hold to be true. Besides the four canonical Gospels, other purported gospels exist, which the Church has long recognized as non-canonical, meaning not inspired by God and thus not guaranteed to be trustworthy accounts of what Jesus actually said and did. This is because the books did not fit the criteria used by the early Church to determine which books were inspired by the Holy Spirit—their language was different, their teachings weren't consistent with the known teachings of the Apostles, and they were written *after* all the canonical books (usually after the first century).

Some of the non-canonical "gospels" sought to undermine the Christian faith. Among these were the gnostic gospels. Written by the gnostic sects, which flourished between the second and fourth centuries, these books deny that Jesus was a real man and that he died for the salvation of the world. Because they are outside of the canon, they are often referred to as the apocryphal gospels, although, in reality, they are not gospels at all because they do not actually teach the Good News.

That being said, there also are non-canonical books that can be useful because they provide historical context for the periods in which they were written. Some also contain information that may be true, such as the *Protoevangelium of James*, which mentions the names of Mary's parents (Anne and Joachim). There also are other early texts that are neither gospels nor part of the canon, but which still give us important information about the early Church. One such book is the *Didache*, or *The Teaching of the Apostles*, which is an early manual of the Church. It describes Baptism, parts of the Mass, moral teachings of the Apostles, and liturgical seasons, offering valuable insights into the life and worship of the first Christians.

We don't read these non-canonical sources with the same reverence as we do Sacred Scripture, nor do we consider them to have the same authority. Nevertheless, as historical documents, they still offer important contributions to our understanding of the Gospel itself.

The Gospel Story

The Gospels of Matthew, Mark, Luke, and John are unique in that they each reveal something about the life and mission of Jesus Christ that no other Gospel does. They all show us the Good News unfolding from a slightly different angle. We'll spend some time looking at those differences in the next section of this book. First, though, it's important to reflect upon what they have in common, what—or, more accurately, who—sits at the heart of each Gospel: Jesus Christ himself.

At the time Jesus was born, Judea was both better off and worse off than it had been for many years. For almost a hundred years, from the Maccabean revolt in the mid-second century BC until the mid-first century BC, the Jewish people finally had their long sought-after independence. A Jewish king, who was also a high priest, sat upon the throne. The temple had been rebuilt and was a flourishing center for both worship and trade. At first glance, it seemed as if God had finally honored his promise and restored the Kingdom of David. But all was not as it seemed.

The king who sat upon the throne was a Levite, not a descendant of David. The ten lost tribes had not been brought back into Israel, and the Samaritans who lived in the north hated their Jewish rulers, who had destroyed the altars they had built for false gods. The Judea of this time period was a man-made kingdom, not a divine one, and like all man-made kingdoms, it collapsed. In 63 BC, the Roman army conquered the small nation. They allowed the Levite kings to remain on the throne for a time, but in 40 BC they helped a powerful Edomite named Herod overthrow the old kings and take control of Jerusalem.

Herod paid the Romans back by taxing the Jewish people heavily and sending the money as tribute to Rome. He also renovated the temple on a grand scale, subsidized the temple priests, and imitated King Solomon by taking multiple wives. Herod, seems to have thought that the Davidic kingdom had been restored under him. But the majority of the Jews disagreed. They knew the promised Messiah and the promised restoration had yet to come. So, they kept on waiting.

The Incarnation

Unbeknownst to anyone but a young Jewish girl named Mary, that waiting ended not long before the fortieth year of Herod's reign. In her home in Nazareth, an angel named Gabriel appeared to Mary and told her that she would be the mother of a very special child, the Son of the Most High, who would be given the throne of David and would reign over Jacob (Israel) forever (Luke 1:26–38). As Isaiah had foretold long ago, Mary was a virgin. She was betrothed to a man named Joseph, but not yet married. Joseph, a good and just man, bowed to the will of God and agreed to be a foster father to Mary's remarkable child.

In a stable in Bethlehem, the City of David, Mary gave birth to her son, Jesus. The angels rejoiced and announced the news to the little and the least of the kingdom: poor shepherds working in a field. Later, when Jesus' parents presented him at the temple in Jerusalem, an aging prophet named Simeon and an aging prophetess named Anna both recognized the child as the child of the Promise, the one for whom they had been waiting. Wise men from the East also, by the grace of God, interpreted a sign in the heavens to determine that a child who would become a great king had been born. They traveled to find him, bringing gifts of gold (a gift fit for a king), incense (a gift fit for a priest), and myrrh (an oil used to anoint the dead before burial). Their travels, unfortunately, brought them in contact with Herod, who believed the child would threaten his dynasty. Accordingly, Herod ordered the execution of all Jewish males in Bethlehem under the age of two.

To save their child, Joseph and Mary fled to Egypt, recalling the flight Jacob and his descendants made to save themselves from famine. And after Herod's death, they, too, came out of Egypt and returned to the Promised Land. In Nazareth they made their home, with Joseph working as a carpenter and Jesus working by his side. These were the hidden years, with little known about the life of Jesus other than his disappearance at the age of twelve, when his parents were on pilgrimage in Jerusalem. They found him, after three days, teaching his elders in the Temple.

Jesus' Public Ministry

Finally, around age thirty, Jesus began the public phase of the work he came to earth to do. He gathered a group of twelve disciples and began intensely teaching them about who he was and what God wanted for and from them. Just as God had formed a people so that they could receive his Son, Jesus formed a group of disciples so that they could receive the fullness of truth and share it with others. These disciples were watching by his side as he taught and prayed, healed and suffered. They saw him condemn the Jewish rulers who expected people to live by rules that they didn't live by themselves. They saw him reach out to the outcasts—to tax collectors, prostitutes, and non-Jews. And they saw him work miracles that almost had to be seen to be believed. Because of Jesus, the blind saw, the deaf heard, the lame walked, the sick grew healthy, and the dead returned to life. Water also turned to wine, and a few fishes and loaves of bread became feasts for thousands.

Most of all, the twelve disciples heard Jesus preach. They heard him talk about the kingdom of God. They heard him teach people how to fast privately and pray boldly, addressing God as "Our Father." They also heard him call the little, the poor, the meek, the grieving, the persecuted, and the humble "blessed" and promise the kingdom to them. Then, they heard him say that those who wanted to enter the kingdom needed to be "born of water." Even more shockingly, they heard him say that unless one ate Jesus' flesh and drank his blood, they could have no life in them.

As three years quickly passed, the disciples likewise witnessed him say that the two greatest commandments were to love God with your whole heart, mind, soul, and strength, and to love your neighbor as yourself. Those neighbors, he then explained, weren't just friends and fellow Jews, but all men and women. In the disciples' presence, Jesus challenged people to honor the poor, love their enemies, and forgive anyone who hurt them, not just one time or seven times, but repeatedly, always.

Jesus said many more things, much of which the Apostles couldn't understand. He talked about the world ending and the temple being destroyed. He changed the name of one disciple from Simon to Peter, because Peter meant rock and Jesus had said Peter would be the rock upon which he would build his Church. He entrusted Peter with the keys to the kingdom, and gave him the power to bind and loose, forgive sins, and make judgments. He shocked people by claiming the Divine Name, I AM, as his own, and said that the Father and he were one, that anyone who had seen him had seen the Father. Voices that spoke from clouds confirmed this, calling Jesus God's Beloved Son and urging people to listen to him. The poor adored him. The authorities hated him.

Through all this, what Jesus *didn't* talk about was overthrowing the Romans or kicking Herod off his throne. Instead, he talked about suffering and dying and rising again on the third day. There was no planned revolution, at least not in the way men and armies think of such things. Rather, there was a planned sacrifice.

The Paschal Mystery

Three years into Jesus' public ministry, the time for that sacrifice had come. On the Sunday before the Passover, he entered Jerusalem in triumph, riding on a donkey as Solomon did before his coronation, with the people crying out "Hosanna" and praising him as the Son of David. Soon afterwards, one of his disciples, Judas, promised to lead the Jewish authorities to Jesus in exchange for thirty pieces of silver. Judas would make it easy for them to arrest Jesus, in the dead of night, when he was most vulnerable.

But first, during the Feast of the Passover, Jesus' disciples, including Judas, ate with him in the Upper Room. There, Jesus consecrated bread and wine, called them his Body and Blood, and commanded the disciples to do this in memory of him. He also washed their feet, said they were to follow his example, and promised that he would send the Holy Spirit to guide them. Then, Jesus and the Apostles left to pray in the Garden of Gethsemane on the Mount of Olives.

There, Jesus was arrested, his location betrayed by one of the Twelve, Judas, who had snuck away from the others. He was tried first in the dead of night by the Jewish authorities, then taken to the Roman governor Pilate. While some had greeted him with praise and palm branches the Sunday before, now others cried out for his death. So Pilate, anxious to prevent a revolt, ordered Jesus to be crucified. He was beaten, mocked, tortured, and made to carry the wood upon which he would die up the hill to his place of execution. Once there, he hung upon a cross, between two thieves, with only his mother, one Apostle, and a few female friends still standing by his side. The rest of his disciples had abandoned him, afraid of suffering the same fate.

Finally, as the Jews were observing the festival of Passover, Jesus died. His last words were words of forgiveness for his tormentors, concern for his mother, and cries to his Father in heaven. He gave up his Spirit, the earth shook, and the veil of the Temple, which secured the Holy of Holies, was torn in two. He was buried quickly in a nearby tomb before the Sabbath rest began.

But death wasn't the end for Jesus. On Sunday, the third day since the day of his crucifixion according to Jewish calculation, he rose again. He then walked among the living with a body and wounds that his disciples could touch and see. He ate. He drank. He lived in his physical body among men. For forty days he remained with his Apostles, helping them to understand what his life and death had really meant. He helped them see that he was God the Son, fully man and fully God. He helped them understand that he had offered himself as a sacrifice to atone for the sins of the world. And through it all, he helped them recognize how, at long last, every covenant promise of the Old Covenant had been fulfilled.

Promises Fulfilled

On the cross, Jesus had born the covenant curses for every man, woman, and child who had ever or would ever live. He had been the obedient son that Adam refused to be, and now the gates of heaven were open to humanity once more. The new creation prefigured in the time of Noah could truly come to be. The great blessing to all the world promised to Abraham through his descendants had come at last. Like Moses, he had come to lead the people out of slavery to sin; and, just as passing through the Red Sea had brought deliverance to Israel, now Baptism would bring deliverance to all who received it. Jesus' calling as Priest, Prophet, and King—the same calling God gave to Israel before they worshipped the golden calf—would now be given to everyone who joined themselves to him in Baptism. He would reign forever over the restored Kingdom of David, the kingdom of God, and all who followed him would have a place in that kingdom.

Forty days after his Resurrection, Jesus commanded the Apostles to invite people into that kingdom on Earth: the Church. He told them to baptize people in the name of the Father and the Son and the Holy Spirit, making disciples of all men and women, in all nations, by teaching, preaching, and the sacraments. Then, Jesus ascended into heaven, promising that someday, at the end of days, he would return.

That is the true story the Gospels tell us. That is the Good News they bring. That is the account of Jesus' life handed on by his Apostles, first through their words and then through their writing. How the Apostles did that, though, and what they emphasized, differs from Gospel to Gospel, with each Gospel bringing its own light to illuminate the fullness of who Jesus was. So now let's look more closely at those individual lights.

SELECTED READING:
Benedict XVI, *Verbum Domini*, nos. 94–95

Since the entire People of God is a people which has been "sent," the Synod reaffirmed that "the mission of proclaiming the word of God is the task of all of the disciples of Jesus Christ based on their Baptism." No believer in Christ can feel dispensed from this responsibility which comes from the fact of our sacramentally belonging to the Body of Christ. A consciousness of this must be revived in every family, parish, community, association and ecclesial movement. The Church, as a mystery of communion, is thus entirely missionary, and everyone, according to his or her proper state in life, is called to give an incisive contribution to the proclamation of Christ.

Bishops and *priests*, in accordance with their specific mission, are the first to be called to live a life completely at the service of the word, to proclaim the Gospel, to celebrate the sacraments and to form the faithful in the authentic knowledge of Scripture. *Deacons* too must feel themselves called to cooperate, in accordance with their specific mission, in this task of evangelization.

Throughout the Church's history *the consecrated life* has been outstanding for explicitly taking up the task of proclaiming and preaching the word of God in the *missio ad gentes* [mission to the nations] and in the most difficult situations, for being ever ready to adapt to new situations and for setting out courageously and boldly along fresh paths in meeting new challenges for the effective proclamation of God's word.

The *laity* are called to exercise their own prophetic role, which derives directly from their Baptism, and to bear witness to the Gospel in daily life, wherever they find themselves. In this regard the Synod Fathers expressed "the greatest esteem, gratitude and encouragement for the service to evangelization which so many of the lay faithful, and women in particular, provide with generosity and commitment in their communities throughout the world, following the example of Mary Magdalene, the first witness of the joy of Easter." The Synod also recognized with gratitude that the ecclesial movements and the new communities are a great force for evangelization in our times and an incentive to the development of new ways of proclaiming the Gospel.

In calling upon all the faithful to proclaim God's word, the Synod Fathers restated the need in our day too for a decisive commitment to the *missio ad gentes*. In no way can the Church restrict her pastoral work to the "ordinary maintenance" of those who already know the Gospel of Christ. Missionary outreach is a clear sign of the maturity of an ecclesial community. The Fathers also insisted that the word of God is the saving truth which men and women in every age need to hear. For this reason, it must be explicitly proclaimed. The Church must go out to meet each person in the strength of the Spirit (cf. *1 Cor* 2:5) and continue her prophetic defense of people's right and freedom to hear the word of God, while constantly seeking out the most effective ways of proclaiming that word, even at the risk of persecution. The Church feels duty-bound to proclaim to every man and woman the word that saves (cf. *Rom* 1:14).

QUESTIONS FOR REVIEW

1. What are the three Synoptic Gospels? what does "synoptic" mean?
2. What are the gnostic "gospels" and what truths did they deny?
3. Describe the relationship each Gospel author had to Christ.
4. Why was the "restoration" of Israel under the Hasmonean dynasty not a real restoration?
5. How did Jesus' life and death fulfill each of the Old Testament covenants?

QUESTIONS FOR DISCUSSION

1. Which of Jesus' teachings are you most attracted to? Why?
2. What aspects of Jesus' teachings are you least attracted to? Why?
3. Does Jesus meet your expectations of what a Savior would look like? Explain. What does people's rejection of him tell us about the world's expectations?

Chapter 2

The Four Gospels

The Gospel of Matthew

|| ASSIGNED READING
|| Matthew 1–7, 10:1–25; 17, 19, 20, 25:14–46; 26–28

The Gospel of Matthew is the first Gospel and the first book in the New Testament canon. Although some scholars believe Mark's Gospel was written prior to Matthew's and dispute Matthew's authorship, the tradition of the Church, handed down by the early Church Fathers, is unanimous that Matthew's Gospel was the first of the four Gospels to be written. Indications in the text that suggest Matthew's Gospel appeared before the destruction of Jerusalem and the Temple in AD 70 lend credence to this tradition. Likewise, early Christian tradition attributes the authorship of the Gospel of Matthew to the Apostle Matthew, the tax collector called by Jesus himself (Matt 9:9).

Matthew's own Jewish upbringing shines through in the text, which has led scholars through the centuries to conclude that Jewish Christians, specifically in Palestine and neighboring areas, were his primary audience. One example of how Matthew's Jewishness shapes the text is his opening genealogy, which traces Jesus' ancestry back to David and

Abraham, connecting him to other covenant mediators and demonstrating that Jesus fulfills God's promises to David in 2 Samuel 7. Likewise, this Gospel is divided into five sections, similar to the Pentateuch, while Matthew's account of the Sermon on the Mount makes constant reference to the Old Testament, noting repeatedly, "You have heard that it was said" (Matt 5:21, 27, 33, 38, 43).

Other examples include Matthew's inclusion of Jesus challenging the Jewish understanding of divorce, allusions to other Old Testament figures and beliefs, Jesus quoting the Jewish Scriptures to the devil during his forty-day fast in the wilderness (which itself recalled the Israelites' forty years in the wilderness), and his account of the Transfiguration, which tells us that Jesus was talking to Moses and Elijah, who represent the law and the prophets in the Jewish tradition.

Perhaps the clearest evidence both of Matthew's Jewish faith and his intended audience is his focus on the kingdom. Throughout his Gospel, Matthew specifically mentions the kingdom of heaven thirty-two times. Among those references are John the Baptist's and Jesus' callings for repentance (Matt 3:2 and 4:17), the Beatitudes (5:3), the encounter with the rich young man (19:23), and when Jesus commissions Peter as the "rock" of the Church (16:19). Matthew likewise drives home the idea that Jesus is the Son of David who will inherit David's throne: he has Jesus enter Jerusalem on Palm Sunday as Solomon once did (riding on a donkey), notes that Pilate inscribed "King of the Jews" on Jesus' cross, and has Jesus quote the psalms of David from the cross.

In all this, Matthew tells his audience that the kingdom of heaven is the kingdom they have been waiting for. This is the kingdom the Son of David will rule forever. But it's not the kingdom they expected. It's a divine kingdom, a heavenly kingdom, which will be open to all the people of the world, including the descendants of the lost ten tribes, who intermarried and disappeared into other nations.

This kingdom, Matthew makes clear by the end of his Gospel, is manifest on earth in the Church. It is in Matthew that we hear Jesus entrust the keys of his kingdom to Peter, echoing words spoken in Isaiah 22:22, when the king of Israel entrusts the keys of his kingdom to his prime minister. It is in Matthew that Jesus tells Peter that he will be the rock upon which Jesus will build his Church. And it is at the end of Matthew that Jesus gives what the Church calls the Great Commission, commanding his disciples to teach and preach and baptize all nations in the name of the Father and of the Son and of the Holy Spirit.

Although many of these details are not included in other Gospels, this doesn't mean that Matthew made them up or was trying to push an agenda. It simply reflects the truth we talked about earlier regarding the authorship of Scripture. The Holy Spirit inspired the human authors, but he didn't have them take dictation. The human authors brought their whole selves to the writing process, including their personalities, personal experiences, and faith.

Matthew's life as a first-century Jew helped him to appreciate the importance of the covenants to the Jews and to understand what the restoration of the kingdom meant to them. He wanted them to see how Jesus fulfilled the covenants and not only restored but transformed the kingdom. So, he included true facts from Jesus' life, death, and Resurrection that could help them see Jesus was the long-awaited Son of David. Because Matthew brought himself to the text, we, today, are able to see and understand Jesus in a way we never would have otherwise.

The same holds true for the Gospel of Mark.

The Gospel of Mark

|| Assigned Reading
|| Mark 1, 4, 11, 14–16

The Gospel of Mark is the shortest Gospel, most likely written in the 60s AD and traditionally attributed to John Mark, whose mother's home in Jerusalem is mentioned in Acts 12:12 as one of the places where the first Christians gathered. John Mark himself traveled on a missionary journey with Ss. Paul and Barnabas, and traveled with St. Peter as well, possibly as an interpreter (Acts 12:25; 13:5; 15:36–39; 1 Pet 5:13). His time with

Peter and the other Apostles would have given him access to a variety of accounts about Jesus' life and works, and he would have been intimately familiar with the oral preaching of the Gospel.

Unlike Matthew, Mark's intended audience seems to be Gentile believers in Rome, who are unfamiliar with Jewish traditions. His Gospel explains Jewish customs, translates Aramaic phrases and words, and at the very climax of his Gospel, after Jesus has breathed his last breath on the cross, it is a Roman soldier who exclaims, "Truly this man was the Son of God!" (Mark 15:39).

Mark's Gospel is divided into two sections. The first half (chapters 1–8) focuses exclusively on Jesus' public ministry. The second half (chapters 8–15) relays the events leading up to Jesus' Passion, death, and Resurrection. The whole of the Gospel moves quickly, almost giving the feeling that Jesus and his Apostles spent three years racing around Galilee and Judea, barely taking time to stop and catch their breath. In part, this is because while Matthew devotes much of his Gospel to Jesus' preaching, Mark is far more interested in what Jesus *did*. One miraculous event quickly follows the next, with Jesus healing people, driving out demons, and calming stormy seas in quick succession. Through all these events Mark demonstrates that Jesus is no mere prophet; he is divine, the Son of Man and the Son of God.

An important focus in the second part of the Gospel is the Fatherhood of God, which, in turn, reinforces the divinity of Jesus. In Mark 8:38, Jesus, in speaking about his death and Resurrection, mentions the "Son of man" and the "glory of his Father." He continues in Mark 11:25 by calling us to forgive so that that our Father in heaven would forgive us. Then he mentions that only the Father knows the hour of the end of days (Mark 13:32). Lastly, and most importantly, in an account demonstrating both his humanity and his divinity, Jesus refers to God as "Abba" (Mark 14:36), which is a familiar and intimate word for "father."

Through it all, Mark makes the case for discipleship. From the responses of love and astonishment in both the crowds that witness his miracles and the people whom Jesus heals, to the Roman centurion's response to Jesus' death on the cross, Mark calls the people of Rome to react with similar astonishment. His goal seems to be for all those who read his Gospel to repeat the centurion's words, "Truly this man was the Son of God!" (Mark 15:39).

The Gospel of Luke

|| ASSIGNED READING
|| Luke 1–4; 6:12–36; 9:1–36; 22–24

Just as Matthew brought his Jewish history to his Gospel and Mark brought his evangelical fervor to his, Luke's Gospel reflects his own upbringing as a non-Jewish Gentile. Scripture tells us that Luke was a physician who accompanied Paul in his later missionary travels during the late 50s and early 60s. He is mentioned by St. Paul in Colossians 4:14, Philemon verse 24, and 2 Timothy 4:11, where he is Paul's only companion during what was likely his first imprisonment in Rome.

A Syrian from the city of Antioch, Luke was exceptionally well educated, with his Gospel reflecting extensive knowledge of both Greek writings and the Greek versions of the Old Testament. He was not, though, as the prologue to his Gospel makes clear, part of the first generation of Christians. He states at the outset that he has received all his knowledge about Jesus from "those who from the beginning were eyewitnesses and ministers of the word" (Luke 1:2). Addressing both his Gospel and the Book of Acts (which he also authored) to Theophilus, Luke then explains that he himself has thoroughly researched the events and has set out to write them in an "orderly fashion" so that Theophilus can have greater certainty about the truths he has heard preached.

Although some scholars hold that Luke was written after the destruction of the Jerusalem Temple in AD 70, the fact that the Book of Acts ends with Paul in prison for the first time, not dead, probably means it was written closer to AD 62. His primary audience was likely Gentile Christians living throughout the Mediterranean region. Evidence for this includes not only the Greek name of the man to whom both his Gospel and Acts are addressed, Theophilus, but also his substitution of Greek names for the Aramaic or Hebrew names (e.g., Luke 23:33; Mark 15:22); his lack of attention for specifically Jewish concerns, like the eating of unclean meat (e.g., Mark 7:1–23); and his mention of Gentiles in both his references and stories, such as Simeon's prayer in Luke 2:30–32, the reference to Naaman the Syrian in 4:27, and the Samaritan leper in 17:11–19. Throughout his Gospel, Luke is intent on showing Gentiles that they, too, have a place in the New Covenant.

More than any other Gospel, Luke's account shows a particular interest in Mary, Jesus' mother. It is because of Luke that we know about the events of the Annunciation and Mary's visit to her cousin Elizabeth, the birth of John the Baptist, and much of the Nativity story. Luke is the one who tells us why Mary and Joseph were in Bethlehem when Jesus was born, that there was no room for them at an inn, that the infant Jesus lay in a manger, and that angels brought news of his birth to shepherds, who came to pay homage to him. Luke is also the one who relays the stories of the presentation of Jesus in the Temple, as well as the finding of Jesus in the Temple at age twelve.

In addition to Luke's exacting concern for the historical facts of Jesus' birth and family, Luke also focuses on Jesus' role as Savior of all people. By including Mary's prayer in 1:52–53—"he has put down the mighty from their thrones, and exalted those of low degree; he has filled the hungry with good things, and the rich he has sent empty away"—Luke announces this theme from the very outset of his Gospel. He then continually reinforces it, showing Jesus tending to those considered the least important in his day, including widows (Luke 7:11–15), lepers (17:12), the poor (21:3), and those considered unclean (8:43–47).

Luke shows us Jesus' mercy and compassion by including accounts of Jesus embracing sinners (Luke 7:41–47) and the parable of the Good Samaritan (10:29–37). He shows us the importance of the Spirit in the life of the Christian through repeated references to him (1:35; 2:25–27; 4:1, 18; 10:21; 11:13; 24:49). And Luke drives home the importance of prayer through frequently showing us Jesus himself praying, retreating to quiet places to pray, and urging his disciples to be persistent in their prayers (3:21; 5:16; 6:12; 9:28; 18:1–8).

Lastly, Luke's Gospel highlights the centrality of the Eucharist to the New Covenant. Although all four Gospels mention the Eucharist, and all three Synoptic Gospels recall the institution of the sacrament at the Last Supper, only the Gospel of Luke mentions the term "New Covenant" in that institution narrative (Luke 22:20). Later, after the Resurrection, Luke recounts how a group of disciples didn't recognize the resurrected Christ until "he took the bread and blessed and broke it, and gave it to them." Then, he continues, "their eyes were opened and they recognized him" (24:30–31). "[He] was known to them in the breaking of the bread," they later tell the other disciples (24:35), showing us that the Eucharist is the sign of the New Covenant, the constant reminder of Christ's faithfulness and ongoing presence in our midst.

The Gospel of John

|| ASSIGNED READING
|| John 1–4; 6–8:20; 9–10:19; 11:1–19; 13–21

The Gospel of John, also known as the Fourth Gospel, is the only Gospel that names its author within the text; John 21:24 tells us that it was written by the Beloved Disciple. Although the Gospel doesn't identify exactly who the Beloved Disciple is, the Church has good reason to believe it is the Apostle John, the son of Zebedee. She bases this claim partly on textual evidence: the Gospel's author was clearly not only an Apostle and an eyewitness to the events, but also seems to have been one of Jesus' innermost circle of Peter, James, and John. Since Peter is distinguished from the Beloved Disciple elsewhere in the Gospel (John 21:20), and James' martyrdom predates the Gospel's authorship, that leaves John. Strong support for this interpretation comes from the earliest Church Fathers, who all attribute the Fourth Gospel to the Apostle John. This includes St. Irenaeus (born in AD 130), who was a disciple of St. Polycarp, who himself was a companion and disciple of St. John.

The Gospel was written for an audience of Mediterranean Jews and Jewish Christians sometime before the end of the first century AD. Most scholars date it to sometime in the 90s, although some evidence within the text suggests an even earlier date, possibly prior to the destruction of the Temple in AD 70.

Traditionally, scholars have divided the Gospel into two "books": the Book of Signs and the Book of Glory. The Book of Signs comprises much of the first half of John's Gospel—John 1:19–12:50—and focuses on Jesus' public ministry. It contains seven explicitly named "signs," each of which, in some way, attests to Jesus' divinity. They are:

1. The miracle at Cana (John 2:1–11);
2. The healing of the official's son (John 4:46–54);
3. The healing of the paralytic (John 5:1–9);
4. The multiplication of the loaves (John 6:1–14);
5. The restoration of the blind man (John 9:1–41);
6. The raising of Lazarus (John 11:17–44); and, most important of all,
7. The Resurrection of Jesus. (This is actually the second sign mentioned in the Gospel—John 2:18–22—but is the final and climactic sign to be accomplished—John 20:1–10.)

The Book of Glory comprises much of the second half of John's Gospel—John 13:1–20:31—and focuses on the events of Holy Thursday through Easter Sunday. It begins with the Last Supper, in which Jesus gives the example of washing the feet of his disciples (John 13), promises them the Holy Spirit (John 14), and prays for the Church in what is known as his "high priestly prayer" (John 17). It then continues with the account of his Passion, and Jesus entrusting Mary to the Beloved Disciple and the Beloved Disciple to Mary (John 19:26–27). Here, the Beloved Disciple represents all believers and, as such, calls all of us who follow Jesus to cultivate a relationship with Mary as well. After Jesus' death, water and blood pour out from his side (John 19:34), which the Church Fathers believed signified the Baptism and the Eucharist. The Book of Glory concludes with the Resurrection and mentions of Jesus' appearances to the Apostles. John tells us:

Now Jesus did many other signs in the presence of the disciples, which are not written in this book; but these are written that you may believe that Jesus is the Christ, the Son of God, and that believing you may have life in his name. (John 20:30–31)

The Gospel then includes one more chapter, in which Jesus entrusts his Church to Peter.

Throughout the entirety of his Gospel, John highlights Jesus' divinity. That is, he makes it clear that Jesus isn't just a holy man or a wise man; he is God himself, come to earth to save us. This focus starts at the beginning, when John echoes the opening passages of the Book of Genesis in his own opening lines. Note the similarities in the passages below:

In the beginning...

Genesis 1:1–5	John 1:1–5
In the beginning God created the heavens and the earth. The earth was without form and void, and darkness was upon the face of the deep; and the Spirit of God was moving over the face of the waters. And God said, "Let there be light"; and there was light. And God saw that the light was good; and God separated the light from the darkness. God called the light Day, and the darkness he called Night. And there was evening and there was morning, one day.	In the beginning was the Word, and the Word was with God, and the Word was God. He was in the beginning with God; all things were made through him, and without him was not anything made that was made. In him was life, and the life was the light of men. The light shines in the darkness, and the darkness has not overcome it.

Jesus, John tells us, is the Word, through which all creation came to be (John 1:14). He was with God and he is God. John also makes it clear to us that Jesus knew this; Jesus hadn't forgotten his divine identity when he came to earth. He knew who he was, he told others who he was, and he suffered for that. One of the ways John communicates this to us is through Jesus' "I AM" statements.

Remember in Exodus 3, when God appeared to Moses and declared, "I AM WHO I AM"? With those words, God revealed his name to Moses. That revelation was a gift, a sign of God's intimacy with his people; the unknown, mysterious God of the universe had shared his name with men. The Israelites saw that revelation, in a sense, as a sacred trust. God had given them his name and they, in turn, needed to treat it rightly. They needed to revere it. Accordingly, although they would write out the name of God (as YHWH), they would never speak it. They thought the name too holy to speak. Then, Jesus came along.

Repeatedly, Jesus begins explanations about who he is with the words "I am." He declares, "I am" the "bread of life" (John 6:35), the "light of the world" (John 8:12), the "door of the sheep" (John 10:7), the "Good Shepherd" (John 10:11), the "resurrection and the life" (John 11:25), "the way, and the truth, and the life" (John 14:6), and the "true vine" (John 15:1). Then, in John 8:58, Jesus says to them, "Truly, truly, I say to you, before Abraham was, I am." To our twenty-first-century ears, that may not sound like much. But to first-century Jews, that sounded like blasphemy. It sounded like Jesus saying, "I am God" . . . which is indeed exactly what he was saying.

John's Gospel is unique in that it fleshes out our picture of Jesus' life on earth. Most likely written after the three Synoptic Gospels, John seems intent on including details left out of the others. His privileged place in Jesus' inner circle also gave him access to encounters and events that the other Gospel writers did not have. His Gospel shows how deeply John had pondered his time with Jesus and the meaning of the events he witnessed. Despite the Gospel's beauty and depth, however, some people through the centuries have misused certain passages it contains (for example, John 19:15–16) to attack our Jewish brothers and sisters. This is both contrary to the teaching of the Church and to any proper understanding of Jesus' atoning death.

As the Church explains in the declaration *Nostra Aetate* at the Second Vatican Council:

True, the Jewish authorities and those who followed their lead pressed for the death of Christ; still, what happened in His passion cannot be charged against all the Jews, without distinction, then alive, nor against the Jews of today. Although the Church is the new people of God, the Jews should not be presented as rejected or accursed by God, as if this followed from the Holy Scriptures. All should see to it, then, that in catechetical work or in the preaching of the word of God they do not teach anything that does not conform to the truth of the Gospel and the spirit of Christ.

Furthermore, in her rejection of every persecution against any man, the Church, mindful of the patrimony she shares with the Jews and moved not by political reasons but by the Gospel's spiritual love, decries hatred, persecutions, displays of anti-Semitism, directed against Jews at any time and by anyone.[1]

In short, while some of the Jewish people of Jesus' day persecuted Jesus, other Jews were his closest followers and the first Christians. Jesus Christ himself was a Jew, as were the Blessed Mother, St. Joseph, and all the first Christians.

Ultimately, Jesus died for all our sins—not just the sins of Israel or his Jewish contemporaries. Our sins are as much responsible for the need for his atoning death as those of the Sanhedrin in the first century. Every single one of us bears some of the blame . . . just as every single one of us stands to benefit from Jesus' willing sacrifice of himself on the cross. Ultimately, Christ laid his life down for us. No man took it from him. It was a free gift offered for the salvation of the world. The only possible response to that gift is to love Jesus in return.

---

[1] Second Vatican Council, Declaration on the Relation of the Church to Non-Christian Religions *Nostra Aetate* (October 28, 1965), §4.

SELECTED READING:
Second Vatican Council, *Dei Verbum*, nos. 17–19

The Word of God, which is the power of God for salvation to everyone who has faith (cf. Rom. 1:16), is set forth and displays its power in a most wonderful way in the writings of the New Testament. For when the time had fully come (cf. Gal. 4:4), the Word became flesh and dwelt among us full of grace and truth (cf. Jn. 1:14). Christ established on earth the kingdom of God, revealed his Father and himself by deeds and words; and by his death, resurrection and glorious ascension, as well as by sending the Holy Spirit, completed his work. Lifted up from the earth he draws all men to himself (cf. Jn. 10:32, Gk. text), for he alone has the words of eternal life (cf. Jn. 6:68). This mystery was not made known to other generations as it has now been revealed to his holy apostles and prophets by the Holy Spirit (cf. Eph. 3:4–6, Gk. text), that they might preach the Gospel, stir up faith in Jesus Christ and the Lord, and bring together the Church. The writings of the New Testament stand as a perpetual and divine witness to these realities.

It is common knowledge that among all the inspired writings, even among those of the New Testament, the Gospels have a special place, and rightly so, because they are our principal source for the life and teaching of the Incarnate Word, our Saviour.

The Church has always and everywhere maintained, and continues to maintain, the apostolic origin of the four Gospels. The apostles preached, as Christ had charged them to do, and then, under the inspiration of the Holy Spirit, they and others of the apostolic age handed on to us in writing the same message they had preached, the foundation of our faith: the fourfold Gospel, according to Matthew, Mark, Luke and John.

Holy Mother Church has firmly and with absolute constancy maintained and continues to maintain, that the four Gospels just named, whose historicity she unhesitatingly affirms, faithfully hand on what Jesus, the Son of God, while he lived among men, really did and taught for their eternal salvation, until the day when he was taken up (cf. Acts 1:1–2). For, after the ascension of the Lord, the apostles handed on to their hearers what he had said and done, but with that fuller understanding which they, instructed by the glorious events of Christ and enlightened by the Spirit of truth, now enjoyed. The sacred authors, in writing the four Gospels, selected certain of the many elements which had been handed on, either orally or already in written form, others they synthesized or explained with an eye to the situation of the churches, the while sustaining the form of preaching, but always in such a fashion that they have told us the honest truth about Jesus. Whether they relied on their own memory and recollections or on the testimony of those who "from the beginning were eyewitnesses and ministers of the Word," their purpose in writing was that we might know the "truth" concerning the things of which we have been informed (cf. Lk. 1:2–4).

QUESTIONS FOR REVIEW

1. Who was Matthew and who was his intended audience? What are two ways his Gospel shows us this?
2. Who was Mark and who was his intended audience? What are two ways his Gospel shows us this?
3. Who was Luke and who was his intended audience? What are two ways his Gospel shows us this?
4. Who was John and who was his intended audience? What are two ways his Gospel shows us this?
5. Approximately when were each of the four Gospels written?

QUESTIONS FOR DISCUSSION

1. Which Gospel did you most enjoy reading? Why do you think this particular Gospel spoke more powerfully to you?
2. If you were writing a gospel, would you emphasize Jesus' words, Jesus' deeds, or give both equal attention? Explain.
3. Did the Jesus you encountered in the Gospels surprise you in any way? If so, how? If not, why not?

PART VI

THE NEW TESTAMENT, PART II

Chapter 1

ACTS OF THE APOSTLES

|| ASSIGNED READING
|| Acts 1–2; 5:33–42; 6–8:8; 9:23–10; 13:1–3; 15:1–21;
|| 16:16–40; 17:16–34; 27–28

Authorship, Setting, and Primary Themes

Like the Gospel of Luke, the Acts of the Apostles was written by to St. Luke, the physician who traveled with St. Paul. He addresses Acts to the same man to whom he addressed his Gospel (Theophilus), shows off his medical knowledge by referencing various medical terms (Acts 9:18; 28:6, 8), and even includes himself in the narrative, using the pronoun "we" while describing various missionary journeys of Paul. Also like his Gospel, the Book of Acts was most likely written in the early 60s—perhaps AD 63—for it includes no mention of the persecution of Christians by Nero in AD 64 or the martyrdom of Ss. Peter and Paul shortly afterward.

The Book of Acts begins where the Gospel of Luke left off, just shortly after the Resurrection, with Jesus' Ascension into heaven and his last command to his Apostles:

But you shall receive power when the Holy Spirit has come upon you; and you shall be my witnesses in Jerusalem and in all Judea and Samaria and to the end of the earth. (Acts 1:8)

That command, in turn, becomes the template for the whole Book of Acts, which traces the development of the early Church, starting with the Apostles giving witness to Jesus in Jerusalem (Acts 2–7), then throughout Judea and Samaria (Acts 8–12), and finally to the ends of the earth (Acts 13 forward). Although some of the Apostles would take the Gospel east into Mesopotamia and south into Africa and Egypt, the "ends of the earth" upon which Luke focuses all belong to the Roman Empire. This is primarily because he was Paul's companion and Paul focused his missionary efforts in the West.

Acts itself is divided into two parts. The first part focuses on St. Peter and the early Church in Jerusalem. The second part focuses on St. Paul and his missionary journeys. In its entirety, it covers approximately the first thirty years of the Church's existence, showing how it transformed from a small group of followers in Jerusalem to a growing presence across the Roman Empire. It gives us a glimpse of some of the first theological questions with which the Church wrestled—such as the authority of the first pope, St. Peter; the appointment of successors and helpers for the Apostles; and what aspects of the Jewish law, including dietary restrictions and circumcision, would no longer be observed in the New Covenant. It also shows us the challenges the fledgling Church faced from outside forces—including persecution by both Jewish and Roman leaders, skepticism from the people they sought to evangelize, and the hardships of travel in the first century.

Anointed by the Spirit

The first burst of growth experienced by the Church occurred fifty days after Easter Sunday. When Jesus ascended into heaven, he promised he would send the Holy Spirit to guide and strengthen his followers. The Apostles then spent the next nine days waiting and praying for Jesus to fulfill that promise. Finally, on the Feast of Pentecost, as Jesus' mother Mary and his closest followers gathered in the same room where they had celebrated the Last Supper, the Holy Spirit came. The Book of Acts tells us he descended upon them like tongues of fire. As he did, he filled them with knowledge, wisdom, understanding, counsel, piety, fortitude, and fear of the Lord.

This wasn't the first time the Apostles had encountered the Holy Spirit. They also had witnessed him descending like a dove on Jesus, when he was baptized by John the Baptist. That day, just as prophets had anointed Israel's kings of old, John, in a sense, anointed Christ the King. Later, the Apostles had heard Jesus speak of the Spirit. Not until Pentecost, however, did they fully understand who he was—the third Person of the Holy Trinity—and what his mission was on earth. The Compendium to the Catechism of the Catholic Church explains:

> Fifty days after the Resurrection at Pentecost the glorified Jesus Christ poured out the Spirit in abundance and revealed him as a divine Person so that the Holy Trinity was fully manifest. The mission of Christ and of the Spirit became the mission of the Church which is sent to proclaim and spread the mystery of the communion of the Holy Trinity. . . .

> The Spirit builds, animates and sanctifies the Church. As the Spirit of Love, he restores to the baptized the divine likeness that was lost through sin and causes them to live in Christ the very life of the Holy Trinity. He sends them forth to bear witness to the Truth of Christ and he organizes them in their respective functions so that all might bear "the fruit of the Spirit" (Galatians 5:22). (144–145)

After the Holy Spirit came upon the Apostles, they immediately were inspired to go out into the streets of Jerusalem and begin proclaiming the Gospel. Here, it's important to note two things. First, before Pentecost, the majority of the Apostles weren't what you would call "bold." They ran from Jesus when he was arrested, and (with the exception of St. John) hid while Jesus hung upon the cross. Even after Jesus' Resurrection, they weren't running out into the streets to preach. Not until the Holy Spirit came upon them did they have the courage they needed to carry out the mission entrusted to them by Jesus.

The second fact we need to note is that the feast of Pentecost was a Jewish feast before it was a Christian one. So, on the day the Holy Spirit came to the Apostles, Jerusalem was packed with Jews who had traveled to the city from across the Roman Empire. These visitors spoke different languages, and yet, when the Apostles began preaching the Good News, everyone understood them. Thousands of years before, man's disobedience at Babel led to people being scattered and languages being confused. Now, because of Jesus' obedience, the opposite was happening. The people were being gathered back together in Christ. Unity was being restored.

Growing Pains

The picture that Luke paints of what followed from there is of a community committed to loving God and their neighbors through prayer, works of mercy, and the sacraments. Describing this experience of *communio* he writes:

> And they held steadfastly to the apostles' teaching and fellowship, to the breaking of the bread and to the prayers. And fear came upon every soul; and many wonders and signs were done through the apostles. And all who believed were together and had all things in common; and they sold their possessions and goods and distributed them to all, as any had need. And day by day, attending the temple together and breaking bread in their homes, they partook of food with glad and generous hearts, praising God and having favor with all the people. And the Lord added to their number day by day those who were being saved. (Acts 2:42–47)

As the small community of Christians continued to grow, several challenges presented themselves. First, Peter and the Apostles alone couldn't meet all the people's needs. Among their numbers were widows, orphans, and the poor, who needed special assistance (and weren't always getting it). To solve this problem the Apostles appointed the first deacons to help deal with some of the Church's administrative and personal needs.

Later, disputes arose between those who believed that newly baptized Christians needed to observe all Jewish laws, including circumcision and dietary restrictions. Eventually, this question was resolved at the first council of the Church: the Council of Jerusalem. In Acts 15, the Apostles gathered together to settle these questions. They didn't all agree at first, and different sides made their case. Ultimately, Peter, as the pope, made the decision that many observances of the Old Law had no place in the New Covenant. He explained, "Now therefore why do you make trial of God by putting a yoke upon the neck of the disciples which neither our fathers nor we have been able to bear? But we believe that we shall be saved through the grace of the Lord Jesus, just as they will" (Acts 15:10–11).

At the Council of Jerusalem, arguing against imposing circumcision and the rituals of the Mosaic Law upon new Gentile Christians, was a man named Paul. Paul was not one of the original Twelve Apostles. Rather, Paul was a Pharisee and one of the chief persecutors of the early Christians. But one day as he was traveling to Damascus (and still went by his Hebrew name, Saul), a voice spoke to him, asking, "Saul, Saul, why do you persecute me?" Saul fell to the ground and asked, "Who are you, Lord?" The voice responded, "I am Jesus, whom you are persecuting; but rise and enter the city, and you will be told what you are to do" (Acts 9:4–6). Saul got the message. He went to the Christians, earned their trust, was baptized, and soon began preaching the Gospel with the same fervor with which he had once persecuted the Church. Known from this point forward as Paul, he quickly became the enemy of his former allies (Acts 9:23–25).

The rest of Acts focuses on Paul's multiple missionary journeys. In the decades that followed his conversion, he would travel throughout the Mediterranean world, preaching Christ. As a Roman citizen, highly educated and fluent in Greek, Paul was especially suited to proclaim the Gospel to the Gentiles. Likewise, he knew both Jewish traditions and Greek traditions, so he could help people see the connections between the God of Israel and the Gentile's own desire for truth. Paul's travels were filled with challenges: he was persecuted by believers and nonbelievers alike, beaten, imprisoned, shipwrecked, and eventually martyred in Rome. Yet he persevered, using his brilliant mind and passionate heart to spread the Gospel not only across the Roman Empire, but across time as well, with his many letters to early Christian communities helping countless generations, including our own, to know Christ.

It is to those letters that we now turn.

SELECTED READING:
Pope Benedict XVI, General Audience, April 18, 2012

After the great celebrations let us now return to the Catecheses on Prayer. At the Audience before Holy Week we reflected on the figure of the Blessed Virgin Mary and her prayerful presence among the Apostles while they were waiting for the descent of the Holy Spirit. The Church took her first steps in an atmosphere of prayer. Pentecost is not an isolated episode because the Holy Spirit's presence and action never cease to guide and encourage the Christian community as it journeys on.

Indeed, in addition to recounting the event of the great outpouring in the Upper Room which occurred 50 days after Easter (cf. Acts 2:1–13), St Luke mentions in the Acts of the Apostles other extraordinary occasions on which the Holy Spirit burst in and which recur in the Church's history. And today I would like to reflect on what has been defined as the "little Pentecost," which took place at the height of a difficult phase in the life of the nascent Church.

The Acts of the Apostles tell that after the healing of a paralytic at the Temple of Jerusalem (cf. Acts 3:1–10), Peter and John were arrested (cf. Acts 4:1) for proclaiming Jesus' Resurrection to all the people (cf. Acts 3:11–26). They were released after a hasty trial, joined their brethren and told them what they had been obliged to undergo on account of the witness they had born to Jesus, the Risen One. At that moment, Luke says, "they lifted their voices together to God" (Acts 4:24). Here St Luke records the Church's most extensive prayer in the New Testament, at the end of which, as we have heard, "the place in which they were gathered together was shaken; and they were all filled with the Holy Spirit and spoke the word of God with boldness" (Acts 4:31).

Before reflecting on this beautiful prayer let us take note of an important basic attitude: when the first Christian community is confronted by dangers, difficulties and threats it does not attempt to work out how to react, find strategies, defend itself or what measures to adopt; rather, when it is put to the test, the community starts to pray and makes contact with God.

And what are the features of this prayer? It is a unanimous, concordant prayer of the entire community which reacts to persecution because of Jesus. In the original Greek St Luke uses the word "*homothumadon*"—"all these with one accord," "in agreement," a term that appears in other parts of the Acts of the Apostles to emphasize this persevering, harmonious prayer (cf. Acts 1:14; 2:46).

This harmony was the fundamental element of the first community and must always be fundamental to the Church. Thus it was not only the prayer prayed by Peter and John, who were in danger, but the prayer of the entire community since what the two Apostles were experiencing did not concern them alone but the whole of the Church.

In facing the persecution it suffered for the cause of Jesus, not only was the community neither frightened nor divided but it was also deeply united in prayer, as one person, to invoke the Lord. I would say that this is the first miracle which is worked when because of their faith believers are put to the test. Their unity, rather than being jeopardized is strengthened because it is sustained by steadfast prayer. The Church must not fear the persecutions which she has been subjected to throughout her history but must always trust, like Jesus at Gethsemane, in the presence, help and power of God, invoked in prayer.

Let us take a further step: what does the Christian community ask God at this moment of trial? It does not ask for the safety of life in the face of persecution, nor that the Lord get even with those who imprisoned Peter and John; it asks only that it be granted "to speak [his] word with all boldness" (Acts 4:29); in other words it prays that it may not lose the courage of faith, the courage to proclaim faith. First, however, it seeks to understand in depth what has occurred, to interpret events in the light of faith and it does so precisely through the word of God which enables us to decipher the reality of the world.

In the prayer it raises to the Lord the community begins by recording and invoking God's omnipotence and immensity: "Sovereign Lord, who did make the heaven and the earth and the sea and everything in them" (Acts 4:24). It is the invocation to the Creator: we know that all things come from him, that all things are in his hands. It is knowledge of this which gives us certainty and courage: everything comes from him, everything is in his hands.

QUESTIONS FOR REVIEW

1. Geographically, how did the Gospel spread in the Book of Acts?
2. Describe the difference in the Apostles before and after Pentecost. What can account for this difference?
3. How is Pentecost related to the events surrounding the Tower of Babel?
4. Why was St. Paul especially suited to spreading the Gospel throughout the Roman Empire? Name at least two advantages he possessed.
5. What was the Council of Jerusalem and what did it decide?

QUESTIONS FOR DISCUSSION

1. Like the Apostles, have you ever felt hesitant to admit you are a Christian? If so, explain what happened.
2. In the world around you, what evidence to you see of the divisions that started at the Tower of Babel? What evidence do you see of the unity created at Pentecost?
3. St. Paul had both the courage to admit he had been wrong in persecuting Christians and the courage to begin proclaiming the Gospel to a hostile world. Why does it take courage to admit you're wrong? Is this easy or difficult for you? Explain.

Chapter 2

The Epistles

Much of what we know about the early Christian's teaching, preaching, and sacramental life comes to us from the letters (or "epistles") written by St. Paul, St. Peter, St. John, St. Jude, and St. James. Many of these letters were written even before the Gospels, and almost all address specific communities of Christians within the Roman Empire. In them we see believers much like ourselves, wanting to love God and honor the commandments, but also struggling with sin and human weakness. The first Christians were as prone to pride, envy, lust, sloth, greed, wrath, and vanity as we are, and the Apostles had to help them overcome those weaknesses, grow in their understanding of the Gospel, and live the lives God wanted them to live. The Apostles also had to contend with factions developing within the communities as Christians disagreed with one another and voiced their preferences for the teachings of some missionaries over others.

Again, we see the same thing in the Church today. But the fact that we're prone to the same weaknesses also means that the letters the Holy Spirit inspired the Apostles to write have just as much to say to us as they did to their first audiences.

The Letter to the Romans

|| ASSIGNED READING
|| Romans 1–3; 5–6:14; 8, 11, 15

In the late 50s, St. Paul was getting ready to travel to Rome for the first time to meet the Christian community there and to prepare for further missionary journeys in the West. Prior to his departure, he wrote the community a letter that both addressed problems they were experiencing (particularly tension between Gentile Christians and Jewish Christians) and outlined his approach to the Gospel. Paul may not have meant his Letter to the Romans to be a theological treatise, but that is how it reads. It is, in fact, his most systematic treatment of the question of salvation and how God worked in time, through a people, to redeem the world.

In particular, Paul focuses on making sure that the Romans understand that salvation is not only for the Jews (or any descendent of Israel at the time), but that it is open to all. This is similar to what we saw in Luke and Acts and gives credence to the idea that St. Luke worked with St. Paul. He mentions that "a hardening has come upon part of Israel, until the full number of Gentiles come in, and so all Israel will be saved" (Rom 11:25–26). He also describes on multiple occasions that "we are justified by faith" (Rom 5:1) and that no human being will be justified in God's sight by "works of the law" (Rom 3:20).

The relationship of grace and works is more fully dealt with here than anywhere else in the Bible. As Paul explains, every good thing we do, we do by God's grace. His grace makes all our good works possible. Yet, at the same time, they are still our good works. We still do them. God doesn't force us to do good any more than he forces us to love him. He gives us the grace to do good and the grace to love, but we must still exercise our freedom to put that grace into action.

Noting that we must consider ourselves "dead to sin and alive to God in Christ Jesus" (Rom 6:11), Paul calls us to live out our freedom in love, being guided by the Spirit, growing in virtue, and proclaiming the Gospel. "Let love be genuine," he writes; "hate what is evil, hold fast to what is good; love one another with brotherly affection; outdo one another in showing honor. Never flag in zeal, be aglow with the Spirit, serve the Lord" (Rom 12:9–11).

The First Letter to the Corinthians

|| ASSIGNED READING
|| 1 Corinthians 1–3, 5, 10–15

St. Paul's First Letter to the Corinthians, most likely written in AD 56, addresses many problems unfolding in the Church in the city of Corinth. It also gives Paul an opportunity to develop teachings about the Eucharist, gifts of the Holy Spirit, and Christ's Resurrection. Paul addresses questions about his authority as an apostle (1 Cor 9), condemns abuses that were taking place in the liturgies in homes (1 Cor 11), discusses how to respond appropriately to the gifts of tongues and prophecy (1 Cor 14), and tackles questions such as whether or not to remarry if one becomes a widow (1 Cor 7), whether or not eating meat sacrificed to idols is wrong in itself or only if it leads others to sin (1 Cor 8), and how to handle dissension within the Church (1 Cor 3).

Referring to that dissension amongst the members of the Church, St. Paul asks the Corinthian Christians collectively, "Do you not know that you are God's temple and that God's Spirit dwells in you? If any one destroys God's temple, God will destroy him. For God's temple is holy, and that temple you are" (1 Cor 3:16–17). Having asked that to the Church as a whole, he moves on to ask each individual person a similar question: "Do you not know that your body is a temple of the Holy Spirit within you, which you have from God? You are not your own; you were bought with a price. So glorify God in your body" (1 Cor 6:19–20).

Paul asks these questions particularly in response to the widespread immorality in the community (1 Cor 5), for which Corinth was famous.

Nevertheless, he calls the Church to be examples by shunning immorality (1 Cor 6:18).

In addition to calling the Corinthians to exercise greater virtue, Paul also calls them to exercise greater reverence in their Eucharistic liturgies He explains that the communion they experience when receiving the Eucharist is not merely a communion with one another, but more fundamentally a communion with Christ's Body and Blood. He then reminds them how the Eucharist is to be celebrated:

> For I received from the Lord what I also delivered to you, that the Lord Jesus on the night when he was betrayed took bread, and when he had given thanks, he broke it, and said, "This is my body which is for you. Do this in remembrance of me." In the same way also the chalice, after supper, saying, "This chalice is the new covenant in my blood. Do this, as often as you drink it, in remembrance of me." For as often as you eat this bread and drink the chalice, you proclaim the Lord's death until he comes.

> Whoever, therefore, eats the bread or drinks the cup of the Lord in an unworthy manner will be guilty of profaning the body and blood of the Lord. Let a man examine himself, and so eat of the bread and drink of the cup. For any one who eats and drinks without discerning the body eats and drinks judgment upon himself. (1 Cor 11:23–29)

Elsewhere, Paul focuses on the relationship between Jesus, the Church, and the Holy Spirit, referring to the Church as the Body of Christ "with many parts" and many gifts. These gifts, which are known as the charisms of the Holy Spirit, are given to each person by "the Spirit for the common good" (1 Cor 12:7). He explains:

> To one is given through the Spirit the utterance of wisdom, and to another the utterance of knowledge according to the same Spirit, to another faith by the same Spirit, to another gifts of healing by the one Spirit, to another the working of miracles, to another

prophecy, to another the ability to distinguish between spirits, to another various kinds of tongues, to another the interpretation of tongues. All these are inspired by one and the same Spirit, who apportions to each one individually as he wills. (1 Cor 12:8–11)

Even greater than these gifts, Paul continues, are faith, hope, and love, with the greatest gift of all being love (1 Cor 13:13).

Lastly, St. Paul focuses on the mystery of the resurrection of the dead, which he explains is absolutely central to the Christian faith because "if there is no resurrection of the dead, then Christ has not been raised; if Christ has not been raised, then our preaching is in vain and your faith is in vain" (1 Cor 15:13–14). Likewise, if there is no credibility to the Resurrection, "then those also who have fallen asleep in Christ have perished" (1 Cor 15:18). Paul then compares Adam and Jesus, referring to Jesus as the New Adam and noting: "For as by a man came death, by a man has come also the resurrection of the dead. For as in Adam all die, so also in Christ shall all be made alive" (1 Cor 15:21–22). This tells us that we will experience the ultimate victory over death in Christ through the Resurrection (1 Cor 15:57).

Other New Testament Letters

St. Paul's Letter to the Romans and his First Letter to the Corinthians are just two of the epistles in the New Testament. The rest are divided into two main groups: the remaining Pauline letters and the Catholic Epistles. The Pauline letters consist of Romans, 1 and 2 Corinthians, Galatians, Ephesians, Philippians, Colossians, 1 and 2 Thessalonians, 1 and 2 Timothy, Titus, Philemon, and Hebrews. Of these, Colossians, Philippians, Ephesians, and Philemon are often referred to as the "captivity epistles" because they were written while Paul was under house arrest or another form of detention. 1 and 2 Timothy and Titus are termed the "pastoral epistles" because their chief concern is with effective pastoral ministry.

The Catholic Epistles, on the other hand, are named that way because they are "universal"—they weren't (or, at least it's believed they weren't) addressed to any one particular community. These epistles are James; 1 and 2 Peter; 1, 2, and 3 John; and Jude.

Highlights from each include:

2 Corinthians	Likely written in the fall of AD 56 (the same year as 1 Corinthians), Paul's Second Letter to the Corinthians defends his calling to preach the Gospel and condemns false apostles who preach something other than the truth of Jesus Christ. Paul also calls the Corinthians to be holy and to see their body as a temple, because in the New Covenant the living presence of God resides in each of them.
Galatians	One of Paul's earliest known epistles, this was written in the early 50s AD and is known as one of Paul's most polemical letters. Rich with references to the Old Covenant, Paul seeks to help the Christians of Galatia understand that Jesus Christ has fulfilled the terms of the Old Covenant and inaugurated a New Covenant in which all the peoples of the earth are called to participate. He also stresses that circumcision does not save, and he implores the Galatians to "walk by the Spirit" and not the flesh (5:16).
Ephesians	Traditionally the Church has attributed the Letter to the Ephesians to St. Paul, although modern scholars often dispute its Pauline authorship. Unlike several other epistles in the New Testament, Ephesians was not written to correct misbehavior or settle disputes. It reads instead like a lyrical mediation on the mystery of Christ and his transformation of the world through the Church. Baptized believers, who are part of this new community, are separated from sin and united with the Trinity—they

have become the children of the Father, the body of the Son, and the temple of the Holy Spirit. Perhaps the letter's most famous chapter, Ephesians 5, compares Christ's relationship to the Church as that of a bridegroom wedded to his bride. This spiritual marriage, in turn, is a sign of how Christian husbands and wives should express their love toward one another in unselfish ways. Topics such as grace, unity, and spiritual warfare are also featured in the letter.

Philippians

Probably written in Rome in the early 60s, Paul's letter to the Philippians is more concerned with encouraging and thanking the Christians of Philippi than it is with doctrine. Primarily, he wants them to continue growing in Christian maturity, following the example of Jesus, who always sought to serve others. Throughout the letter, St. Paul often mentions joy and humility, reminding his readers that "I can do all things in him who strengthens me" (4:13) and urging them to "Rejoice in the Lord always; again I will say, Rejoice" (4:4).

Colossians

The authorship of this letter is disputed by some modern scholars, but most interpreters in the history of the Church have read it as a letter from St. Paul written in Rome in the early 60s. The community he addresses in Colossae was not one he founded, but rather one founded by someone Paul had converted. This person came to Paul, asking for help strengthening his struggling community. Certain "troublemakers"—possibly the Jews of Colossae—were sowing doubts among believers. Paul's response is this letter, rich in apologetics and seeking to clarify the truth of Christian doctrine.

The letter proclaims Jesus Christ as God and head of the Church (1:15–23) and describes what Paul has undergone while serving him. It then declares that we have a new life in Christ that should influence all our actions and enjoins the Colossians to:

> Put to death therefore what is earthly in you: immorality, impurity, passion, evil desire, and covetousness, which is idolatry. . . . Put on then, as God's chosen ones, holy and beloved, compassion, kindness, lowliness, meekness, and patience, forbearing one another and, if one has a complaint against another, forgiving each other; as the Lord has forgiven you, so you also must forgive. And over all these put on love, which binds everything together in perfect harmony. (3:5, 12–14)

1 and 2 Thessalonians

First Thessalonians is one of the earliest New Testament documents, written around AD 50. In the letter, Paul writes and gives thanks for the good things he has heard about the Church in Thessalonica (3:6) and encourages the Christians there to live their lives in expectation of Christ's second coming.

In the beginning of 2 Thessalonians, which was written perhaps a year later, Paul acknowledges that the people are growing in love (1:3), but he finds the need to write more about the coming of Christ. He tells the people "not to be quickly shaken in mind or excited" because the day has not yet come (2:2), and that no one should be idle while awaiting his coming (3:6–12).

1 and 2 Timothy, like Titus, are not written to fledgling communities, but to experienced pastors serving their flocks. Because they have a somewhat different tone and style than Paul's other letters, some have questioned the letters' Pauline authorship. However, the Church Fathers generally attributed 1 and 2 Timothy to Paul, and if they are correct, these were likely written in the mid-60s, shortly before Paul's martyrdom.

1 Timothy in particular provides insights into the hierarchy in the early Church, with Paul giving instructions to Timothy on how to select bishops and deacons (chapter 3) and how prayer should transpire (chapter 2). Encouraging Timothy to be a good leader, Paul writes the following:

1 and 2 Timothy

Let no one despise your youth, but set the believers an example in speech and conduct, in love, in faith, in purity. Till I come, attend to the public reading of Scripture, to preaching, to teaching. Do not neglect the gift you have, which was given you by prophetic utterance when the elders laid their hands upon you. Practice these duties, devote yourself to them, so that all may see your progress. Take heed to yourself and to your teaching; hold to that, for by so doing you will save both yourself and your hearers. (4:12–16)

In 2 Timothy, Paul continues to encourage Timothy in his ministry, giving him more advice full of hope, even amidst trials. Paul includes a thought that can sound like a prophecy for our time:

For the time is coming when people will not endure sound teaching, but having itching ears they will accumulate for themselves teachers to suit their own likings, and will turn away from listening to the truth and wander into myths. As for you, always be steady, endure suffering, do the work of an evangelist, fulfil your ministry. (2 Tim 4:3–5)

Titus	Similar to the letters to Timothy, and written around the same time, Paul instructs Titus, a bishop (1:5), on selecting and ordaining priests, teaching the true Gospel (chapter 2), and helping people to lead holy lives (chapter 3).
Philemon	Paul wrote this letter while he was in prison in the early 60s. It concerns a runaway slave named Onesimus, whom Paul considered "a beloved brother . . . both in the flesh and in the Lord" (v. 16). The letter is addressed to Philemon, Onesimus' owner and a fellow Christian. Although Philemon had the right according to Roman law to punish Onesimus, Paul asks him to greet his former slave as a brother, to not punish him, and to consider releasing him out of mercy.
Hebrews	Of all the letters attributed to St. Paul, the Letter to the Hebrews is the most disputed. While the letter itself makes no claim to Pauline authorship, the Church in the East attributed it to Paul from the earliest times, with the Church in the West eventually following suit. Most scholars today reject the Pauline authorship of Hebrews, but many still hold that it comes from one of Paul's disciples. Regardless, the letter's focus is on how Jesus fulfills Old Testament prophecies by being a high priest, similar to Melchizedek of old (chapters 3–5).

James

Tradition holds that the Letter of James was written by James of Jerusalem, who was a relative of Jesus (see Mark 6:3) and the first bishop of the city. The dating of the letter is sometime in the early 60s, before James' martyrdom. It is addressed to the "twelve tribes in the Dispersion" (1:1), which possibly means Israelite Christians who lived outside of Jerusalem or had recently moved out due to persecution. In this epistle, James recommends that Christians "be doers of the word, and not hearers only" (1:22), treat each other without partiality (chapter 2), and bear suffering with patience (chapter 5). He also stresses that if a person has faith, their faith must be made manifest through their works (chapter 2).

1 and 2 Peter

Traditionally the Church has attributed the two epistles of Peter to Simon Peter, one of the Twelve Apostles chosen by Jesus. This would mean that both were written before about AD 67, when Peter was martyred in Rome. Modern scholars often question the apostolic authorship of one or both of these letters, dating them instead in the late first or early second century AD, but there is not enough evidence for these views to disprove Peter's authorship.

1 Peter calls Christians to live a life of holiness in a hostile and unbelieving world, even to the point of suffering for the sake of righteousness, if necessary (3:14). Peter also encourages believers to witness to their faith when others challenge them (3:15) and to resist the attacks of the devil (5:8–9). Jesus, who suffered despite being innocent of sin, stands as the primary model for all Christian behavior.

2 Peter puts believers on guard against those who teach "destructive heresies" that contradict the teachings of the apostles (2:1). These troublemakers, who

scoff at the Church's belief that Jesus will come again in glory, must not be imitated, since they are bound for destruction when God judges the world. On the positive side, Christians who remain faithful to the apostles' teaching have every grace to escape the corruption of the world, most notably the grace to participate in "the divine nature" of God himself (1:4).

1, 2, and 3 John

Each of these letters, which are traditionally attributed to the Apostle John (and likely written anywhere from the late 60s through the early 90s), seek to encourage hope in the God who is good, even in the face of evil. In 1 John, he acknowledges that people are teaching the wrong Gospel, but despite this, Christians must continue to love one another because "God is love, and he who abides in love abides in God, and God abides in him" (4:16).

2 John also mentions that there are "deceivers" (v. 7), but that Christians should continue to love each other and "abide in the doctrine of Christ" because "he who abides in the doctrine has both the Father and the Son" (v. 9).

In 3 John, which is the shortest letter in the New Testament, John addresses Gaius, mentioning that a man named Diotrephes does not respect John's apostolic authority (v. 9), and saying that Gaius and the faithful should do what is good because "he who does good is of God" (v. 11).

Jude

Traditionally, the Letter of St. Jude is attributed to Judas, a relative of Jesus (see Matt 13:55) and possibly the brother of James of Jerusalem, the author of the Letter of James. Writing sometime in the 50s or 60s, Jude addresses false teachers "who pervert the grace of our God into licentiousness" (v. 4) and who are "grumblers, malcontents, following their own passions, loudmouthed boasters, flattering people to gain advantage" (v. 16). In response to these people, he reminds the Church to be faithful, prayerful, and hopeful in the Lord.

SELECTED READING:
Pope Benedict XVI, General Audience, July 2, 2008

Today I would like to begin a new cycle of Catecheses focusing on the great Apostle St Paul. As you know, this year is dedicated to him, from the liturgical Feast of Sts Peter and Paul on 29 June 2008 to the same Feast day in 2009. The Apostle Paul, an outstanding and almost inimitable yet stimulating figure, stands before us as an example of total dedication to the Lord and to his Church, as well as of great openness to humanity and its cultures. It is right, therefore, that we reserve a special place for him in not only our veneration but also in our effort to understand what he has to say to us as well, Christians of today. In this first meeting let us pause to consider the environment in which St Paul lived and worked. A theme such as this would seem to bring us far from our time, given that we must identify with the world of 2,000 years ago. Yet this is only apparently and, in any case, only partly true for we can see that various aspects of today's social and cultural context are not very different from what they were then.

A primary and fundamental fact to bear in mind is the relationship between the milieu in which Paul was born and raised and the global context to which he later belonged. He came from a very precise and circumscribed culture, indisputably a minority, which is that of the People of Israel and its tradition. In the ancient world and especially in the Roman Empire, as scholars in the subject teach us, Jews must have accounted for about 10 percent of the total population; later, here in Rome, towards the middle of the first century, this percentage was even lower, amounting to three percent of the city's inhabitants at most. Their beliefs and way of life, is still the case today, distinguished them clearly from the surrounding environment; and this could have two results: either derision, that could lead to intolerance, or admiration which was expressed in various forms of sympathy, as in the case of the "God-fearing" or "proselytes," pagans who became members of the Synagogue and who shared the faith in the God of Israel. As concrete examples of this dual attitude we can mention on the one hand the cutting opinion of an orator such as Cicero who despised their religion and even the city of Jerusalem (cf. *Pro Flacco*, 66–69) and, on the other, the attitude of Nero's wife, Poppea, who is remembered by Favius Josephus as a "sympathizer" of the Jews (cf. *Antichità giudaiche* 20, 195, 252); *Vita* 16), not to mention that Julius Caesar had already officially recognized specific rights of the Jews which have been recorded by the above-mentioned Jewish historian Flavius Josephus (cf. *ibid.*, 14,200–216). It is certain that the number of Jews, as, moreover, is still the case today, was far greater outside the land of Israel, that is, in the Diaspora, than in the territory that others called Palestine.

It is not surprising, therefore, that Paul himself was the object of the dual contradictory assessment that I mentioned. One thing is certain: the particularism of the Judaic culture and religion easily found room in an institution as far-reaching as the Roman Empire. Those who would adhere with faith to the Person of Jesus of Nazareth, Jew or Gentile, were in the more difficult and troubled position, to the extent to which they were to distinguish themselves from both Judaism and the prevalent paganism. In any case, two factors were in Paul's favour. The first was the Greek, or rather Hellenistic, culture which after Alexander the Great had become a common heritage, at least of the Eastern Mediterranean and of the Middle East, and had even absorbed many elements of peoples traditionally considered barbarian. One writer of the time says in this regard that Alexander "ordered that all should consider the entire oecumene as their homeland . . . and that a distinction should no longer be made between Greek and barbarian" (Plutarch, *De Alexandri Magni fortuna aut virtute*, 6, 8). The second factor was the political and administrative structure of the Roman Empire which guaranteed peace and stability from Britain as far as southern Egypt, unifying a territory of previously unheard of dimensions. It was possible to move with sufficient freedom and safety in this space, making use, among other things, of an extraordinary network of roads and finding at every point of arrival basic cultural characteristics which, without affecting local values, nonetheless represented a common fabric of unification *super partes* [impartially], so that the Jewish philosopher, Philo of Alexandria, a contemporary of Paul himself, praised the Emperor Augustus for "composing in harmony all the savage peoples, making himself the guardian of peace" (*Legatio ad Caium*, 146–147).

There is no doubt that the universalist vision characteristic of St Paul's personality, at least of the Christian Paul after the event on the road to Damascus, owes its basic impact to faith in Jesus Christ, since the figure of the Risen One was by this time situated beyond any particularistic narrowness. Indeed, for the Apostle "there is neither Jew nor Greek, there is neither slave nor free, there is neither male nor female; for you are all one in Christ Jesus" (Gal 3:28). Yet, even the historical and cultural situation of his time and milieu could not but have had an influence on his decisions and his work. Some have defined Paul as "a man of three cultures," taking into account his Jewish background, his Greek tongue and his prerogative as a *civis romanus* [Roman citizen], as the name of Latin origin suggests. Particularly the Stoic philosophy dominant in Paul's time which influenced Christianity, even if only marginally, should be recalled. Concerning this, we cannot gloss over certain names of Stoic philosophers such as those of its founders, Zeno and Cleanthes, and then those closer to Paul in time such as Seneca, Musonius and Epictetus: in them the loftiest values of humanity and wisdom are found which were naturally to be absorbed by Christianity. As one student of the subject splendidly wrote, "Stoicism . . . announced a new ideal, which imposed upon man obligations to his peers, but at the same time set him free from all physical and national ties, and made of him a purely spiritual being" (M. Pohlenz, *La Stoa*, I, Florence, 2, 1978, pp. 565 f.). One thinks, for example, of the doctrine of the universe understood as a single harmonious body and consequently of the doctrine of equality among all people without social distinctions, of the equivalence, at least in principle, of men and women, and then of the ideal of frugality, of the just measure and self-control to avoid all excesses. When Paul wrote to the Philippians, "Whatever is true, whatever is honourable [. . .] whatever is lovely, whatever is gracious, if there is any excellence, if there is anything worthy of praise, think about these things" (Phil 4:8), he was only taking up a purely humanistic concept proper to that philosophical wisdom.

In St Paul's time a crisis of traditional religion was taking place, at least in its mythological and even civil aspects. After Lucretius had already ruled polemically a century earlier that "religion has led to many misdeeds" (*De rerum natura*, 1, 101, On the Nature of Things), a philosopher such as Seneca, going far beyond any external ritualism, taught that "God is close to you, he is with you, he is within you" (*Epistulae morales* to Lucilius, 41, 1). Similarly, when Paul addresses an audience of Epicurean philosophers and Stoics in the Areopagus of Athens, he literally says: "God does not live in shrines made by man, . . . for in him we live and move and have our being" (Acts 17:24, 28). In saying this he certainly re-echoes the Judaic faith in a God who cannot be represented in anthropomorphic terms and even places himself on a religious wavelength that his listeners knew well. We must also take into account the fact that many pagan cults dispensed with the official temples of the town and made use of private places that favoured the initiation of their followers. It is therefore not surprising that Christian gatherings (*ekklesiai*) as Paul's Letters attest, also took place in private homes. At that time, moreover, there were not yet any public buildings. Therefore Christian assemblies must have appeared to Paul's contemporaries as a simple variation of their most intimate religious practice. Yet the differences between pagan cults and Christian worship are not negligible and regard the participants' awareness of their identity as well as the participation in common of men and women, the celebration of the "Lord's Supper," and the reading of the Scriptures.

In conclusion, from this brief over-view of the cultural context of the first century of the Christian era, it is clear that it is impossible to understand St Paul properly without placing him against both the Judaic and pagan background of his time. Thus he grows in historical and spiritual stature, revealing both sharing and originality in comparison with the surrounding environment. However, this applies likewise to Christianity in general, of which the Apostle Paul, precisely, is a paradigm of the highest order from whom we all, always, still have much to learn. And this is the goal of the Pauline Year: to learn from St Paul, to learn faith, to learn Christ, and finally to learn the way of upright living.

QUESTIONS FOR REVIEW

1. Which of St. Paul's letters addresses the different roles of works and grace in our salvation?
2. In which letter does St. Paul give us the words of consecration for the Eucharist still used in the Holy Mass today?
3. What are the "captivity epistles" and why do we call them this?
4. What are the "pastoral epistles" and why do we call them this?
5. What are the "catholic epistles" and why do we call them this?

QUESTIONS FOR DISCUSSION

1. What are some of the good things you have done this week? How has God helped you to do them?
2. St. Paul advises St. Timothy to ignore people who use his young age as a reason to not listen to him proclaim the Gospel. Do you think this is good advice? Why or why not?
3. In his letter, St. James famously wrote "faith without works is dead." What do you think he meant by that? Have you experienced this or witnessed this in your interactions with other Christians? If so, how?

Chapter 3

THE BOOK OF REVELATION

|| ASSIGNED READING
|| Revelation 1–3, 5, 12, 19, 21

Authorship, Audience, and Themes

Of all the books of the Bible, The Revelation of St. John (also called The Book of Revelation or The Apocalypse) is the most difficult to understand. Over the past two thousand years, theologians, priests, and lay readers of the Bible have wrestled with the book's mysterious references to beasts, lampstands, temples, and angels. St. Jerome, a Doctor of the Church and one of most her most outstanding biblical scholars, said that it has "as many mysteries as words."[1]

The author of the Book of Revelation identifies himself simply as John, although many ancient Christians specify that he's the Apostle John. Other information in the book lends support to this tradition, such as the fact that the churches mentioned in the book are all churches in the region near Ephesus, where John lived and ministered. The book shares some common language and themes with the Apostle's other writings, but not many. This is possibly because the book was written at an

---

[1] Jerome, Letter 53 to Paulinus (AD 394), http://www.newadvent.org/fathers/3001053.htm.

earlier date (perhaps as early as AD 68) or simply because John didn't feel free to add his own personal interpretations to the vision given to him by Jesus.

Regardless, the book begins as a letter addressed to the seven churches of Asia (Ephesus, Smyrna, Pergamum, Thyatira, Sardis, Philadelphia, and Laodicea). The author identifies himself as John and explains that while he was in exile on the island of Patmos, Jesus appeared to him and ordered him to write down everything he saw in a book and send it to the seven churches. Some ancient Syriac manuscripts include more specific information, saying that John was exiled to Patmos by Caesar Nero (who reigned from AD 54–68).

From there, John goes into detail, explaining all that he said and heard in the vision Jesus granted him. His recording of the vision bears a marked resemblance to other examples of apocalyptic literature, which was a type of Jewish religious writing common at the time, filled with cosmic symbolism, visions of heaven, and scenes of judgment. John's book also draws heavily from the Old Testament, with two hundred seventy-eight allusions to the Old Testament in its four hundred-four total verses. Many of those allusions come from the prophetic books, especially Daniel, Ezekiel, Isaiah, and Zechariah.

Interpreting John's Vision

The actual events of the vision range from terrifying scenes of death and destruction—with trumpets blasting, plagues descending upon the earth, and the fall of a great city (identified only as "the harlot city")—to glorious glimpses of the saints worshipping in heaven. There is a beast, which seeks to wreak havoc upon the world, and a lamb, who stands even though he was slain. There is also a woman clothed with the sun and wearing a crown of twelve stars, angels worshipping before the lamb, and countless white-robed saints.

Again, trying to make sense of these events and figures isn't easy. There are countless interpretations of what it all means. Most of those interpretations, however, fit into five broad interpretive views of the

Common Interpretive Views of the Book of Revelation[1]

Book of Revelation.	
Critical View	This view situates the book within the problems of its day, most notably the struggle experienced by believing Christians at the hands of both the Roman and Jewish governments. They also see a promise that God will overcome all who oppose him and his people.
Preterist View	This view also sees the events of Revelation in relationship to the book's historical context, although it holds to a broader interpretation. It sees the events of destruction pointing to the end of the Old Covenant, and the heavenly worship signifying the beginning of the New Covenant and the institution of Christianity as the climax of Salvation History.
Historicist View	This view focuses on all of Salvation History, seeing the successive visions of the book corresponding to successive stages of Christian history.
Idealist View	The idealist view interprets the vision of Revelation as an allegory that dramatizes the spiritual struggles faced by the Church and her members in every age.
Futurist View	This view sees the book as a preview of things to come. On this view, it gives a glimpse of the events that will surround the end of history, when Jesus comes again, and the final judgment. In this sense, it is seen as a book of prophecy, whose words have yet to be fulfilled.

So, what is the correct view? Perhaps, in a sense, all of them. As the *Ignatius Catholic Study Bible* explains:

---

[1] Hahn and Mitch, *The Ignatius Catholic Study Bible: The New Testament*, 491.

Christianity's struggle against the mighty Roman Empire is certainly part of the picture, as are the spiritual challenges to faith and fidelity that confront believers bombarded by the claims of the world. So too, one can hardly deny that Revelation offers a message of ultimate hope that looks ahead to the consummation of history and the heavenly glorification of the saints. Less commonly appreciated is the attention Revelation gives to the First Coming of Christ, whose death and Resurrection constitute the theological basis of the book, as well as the coming of Christ in judgment against unbelieving Jerusalem, which was known to the early Christians as the city "where their Lord was crucified" (11:8).[2]

All this is to say that Revelation is a book that defies simple interpretation. The struggles of believers—Jewish and Christian, past and present—all play out in its pages. Kingdoms have fallen, and kingdoms will fall again. Believers have betrayed Jesus, and believers will betray Jesus again. Christians were persecuted, and Christians will be persecuted again. The Book can't be limited to one time or place. It contains something for all times, which is why the Holy Spirit inspired the book and led the Church to include it in the New Testament.

The Liturgy of Heaven and Earth

What the book does make clear is that the business of heaven is worship. In John's vision, we see the angels and saints worshipping before the throne of the Lamb of God, with incense rising and priests in liturgical robes offering prayers. Moreover, because of John's vision, we learn that the prayers and hymns of heaven are the prayers and hymns of the Mass. Our worship here on earth, at every Catholic Church on every Sunday, is a participation in the worship of heaven, with the words we pray echoing those of Revelation.

---

[2] Hahn and Mitch, *The Ignatius Catholic Study Bible: The New Testament*, 491.

These words include the antiphonal chants in Revelation 4:8, 5:13, and 7:10 ("Holy, holy, holy, is the Lord God almighty"; "To him who sits upon the throne and to the Lamb be blessing and honor and glory and might for ever"; "Salvation belongs to our God and to the Lamb"), as well as the Gloria in 15:3–4. They also include the Alleluia in 19:1, 3, 4, 6; the Sanctus ("Holy, holy, holy") in 4:8; the Great Amen in 19:4 and 22:20; and the invitation to the Marriage Supper of the Lamb in 19:9. From beginning to end, the Book of Revelation is soaked with the language of liturgy, with both the words spoken and the actions taken drawing a clear line between the worship of heaven and the worship of the Church in the Mass.

Last but not least, the Book of Revelation reminds us that all we know now is passing away. One day, there will be "a new heaven and a new earth" (Rev 21:1). Until then, the transformation that will eventually come for all Creation is slowly but surely happening in each of us. The Catechism explains:

> The kingdom has come in the person of Christ and grows mysteriously in the hearts of those incorporated into him, until its full eschatological manifestation. Then all those he has redeemed and made "holy and blameless before him in love" [Eph 1:4], will be gathered together as the one People of God, the "Bride of the Lamb" [Rev 21:9], "the holy city Jerusalem coming down out of heaven from God, having the glory of God" [Rev 21:14]. (CCC 865)

SELECTED READING:
Pope Benedict XVI, General Audience, August 23, 2006

In the last Catechesis we had reached the meditation on the figure of the Apostle John. We had first sought to look at all that can be known of his life. Then, in a second Catechesis, we meditated on the central content of his Gospel and his Letters: charity, love. And today we are still concerned with the figure of John, this time to examine the Seer of the Book of Revelation. And let us immediately note that while neither the Fourth Gospel nor the Letters attributed to the Apostle ever bear his name, the Book of Revelation makes at least four references to it (cf. 1:1, 4, 9; 22:8).

It is obvious, on the one hand, that the author had no reason not to mention his own name, and on the other, that he knew his first readers would be able to precisely identify him. We know, moreover, that in the third century, scholars were already disputing the true factual identity of John of the "Apocalypse."

For the sake of convenience we could also call him "the Seer of Patmos" because he is linked to the name of this island in the Aegean [Sea] where, according to his own autobiographical account, he was, as it were, deported "on account of the word of God and the testimony of Jesus" (Rv 1:9).

It was on Patmos itself, "on the Lord's Day . . . caught up in ecstasy" (Rv 1:10), that John had a grandiose vision and heard extraordinary messages that were to have a strong influence on the history of the Church and of entire Western culture.

For example, from the title of his book—*Apocalypse, Revelation*—the words "apocalypse, apocalyptic" were introduced into our language and, although inaccurately, they call to mind the idea of an incumbent catastrophe.

The Book should be understood against the backdrop of the dramatic experiences of the seven Churches of Asia (Ephesus, Smyrna, Pergamum, Thyatira, Sardis, Philadelphia, Laodicea) which had to face serious difficulties at the end of the first century—persecutions and also inner tensions—in their witness to Christ.

John addresses them, showing acute pastoral sensitivity to the persecuted Christians, whom he exhorts to be steadfast in the faith and not to identify with the pagan world. His purpose is constituted once and for all by the revelation, starting with the death and Resurrection of Christ, of the meaning of human history.

The first and fundamental vision of John, in fact, concerns the figure of the Lamb who is slain yet standing (cf. Rv 5:6), and is placed before the throne on which God himself is already seated.

By saying this, John wants first of all to tell us two things: the first is that although Jesus was killed with an act of violence, instead of falling heavily to the ground, he paradoxically stands very firmly on his own feet because, with the Resurrection, he overcame death once and for all.

The other thing is that Jesus himself, precisely because he died and was raised, henceforth fully shares in the kingship and saving power of the Father. This is the fundamental vision.

On this earth, Jesus, the Son of God, is a defenceless, wounded and dead Lamb. Yet he stands up straight, on his feet, before God's throne and shares in the divine power. He has the history of the world in his hands.

Thus, the Seer wants to tell us: trust in Jesus, do not be afraid of the opposing powers, of persecution! The wounded and dead Lamb is victorious! Follow the Lamb Jesus, entrust yourselves to Jesus, take his path! Even if in this world he is only a Lamb who appears weak, it is he who triumphs!

The subject of one of the most important visions of the Book of Revelation is this Lamb in the act of opening a scroll, previously closed with seven seals that no one had been able to break open. John is even shown in tears, for he finds no one worthy of opening the scroll or reading it (cf. Rv 5:4).

History remains indecipherable, incomprehensible. No one can read it. Perhaps John's weeping before the mystery of a history so obscure expresses the Asian Churches' dismay at God's silence in the face of the persecutions to which they were exposed at that time.

It is a dismay that can clearly mirror our consternation in the face of the serious difficulties, misunderstandings and hostility that the Church also suffers today in various parts of the world.

These are trials that the Church does not of course deserve, just as Jesus himself did not deserve his torture. However, they reveal both the wickedness of man, when he abandons himself to the promptings of evil, and also the superior ordering of events on God's part.

Well then, only the sacrificed Lamb can open the sealed scroll and reveal its content, give meaning to this history that so often seems senseless. He alone can draw from it instructions and teachings for the life of Christians, to whom his victory over death brings the message and guarantee of victory that they too will undoubtedly obtain. The whole of the vividly imaginative language that John uses aims to offer this consolation.

Also at the heart of the visions that the Book of Revelation unfolds, are the deeply significant vision of the Woman bringing forth a male child and the complementary one of the dragon, already thrown down from Heaven but still very powerful.

This Woman represents Mary, the Mother of the Redeemer, but at the same time she also represents the whole Church, the People of God of all times, the Church which in all ages, with great suffering, brings forth Christ ever anew. And she is always threatened by the dragon's power. She appears defenceless and weak.

But while she is threatened, persecuted by the dragon, she is also protected by God's comfort. And in the end this Woman wins. The dragon does not win.

This is the great prophecy of this Book that inspires confidence in us! The Woman who suffers in history, the Church which is persecuted, appears in the end as the radiant Bride, the figure of the new Jerusalem where there will be no more mourning or weeping, an image of the world transformed, of the new world whose light is God himself, whose lamp is the Lamb.

For this reason, although John's Book of Revelation is pervaded by continuous references to suffering, tribulation and tears—the dark face of history—, it is likewise permeated by frequent songs of praise that symbolize, as it were, the luminous face of history.

So it is, for example, that we read in it of a great multitude that is singing, almost shouting: "Alleluia! For the Lord our God the Almighty reigns. Let us rejoice and exult and give him the glory, for the marriage of the Lamb has come, and his Bride has made herself ready" (Rv 19:6–7).

Here we face the typical Christian paradox, according to which suffering is never seen as the last word but rather, as a transition towards happiness; indeed, suffering itself is already mysteriously mingled with the joy that flows from hope.

For this very reason John, the Seer of Patmos, can close his Book with a final aspiration, trembling with fearful expectation. He invokes the definitive coming of the Lord: "Come, Lord Jesus!" (Rv 22:20).

This was one of the central prayers of the nascent Christianity, also translated by St Paul into its Aramaic form: "*Marana tha.*" And this prayer, "Our Lord, come!" (I Cor 16:22) has many dimensions.

It is, naturally, first and foremost an expectation of the definitive victory of the Lord, of the new Jerusalem, of the Lord who comes and transforms the world. But at the same time, it is also a Eucharistic prayer: "Come Jesus, now!" And Jesus comes; he anticipates his definitive coming.

So it is that we say joyfully at the same time: "Come now and come for ever!"

This prayer also has a third meaning: "You have already come, Lord! We are sure of your presence among us. It is our joyous experience. But come definitively!"

And thus, let us too pray with St Paul, with the Seer of Patmos, with the newborn Christianity: "Come, Jesus! Come and transform the world! Come today already and may peace triumph!" Amen!

QUESTIONS FOR REVIEW

1. Who wrote the Book of Revelation? Where and when is it believed they wrote it?
2. What evidence do we have for the book's authorship? Name at least two pieces of evidence.
3. What type of Jewish writing does the Book of Revelation resemble?
4. What are the five most common ways of interpreting the Book of Revelation? Give a short, one sentence explanation of each.
5. What are three things that occur in the Book of Revelation that we hear or see in every Mass?

QUESTIONS FOR DISCUSSION

1. Why do you think God would inspire such a puzzling book of the Bible?
2. Is it easy or difficult for you to see the liturgy in which we participate here on earth as a reflection of and participation in the worship of the saints in heaven? Why or why not?
3. Revelation reminds us that God is making all things new. How, even today, is he making you new?

Appendix

Challenges

Objection 1: Catholics Believe in Things That Are Not Found in the Bible. How Do You Justify That?

Everyone believes religious truths that are not found in the Bible. Protestants, for example, believe in the canon of Scripture—the list of books believed to be inspired by the Holy Spirit—but that list isn't found anywhere in the Bible. There's no book of the Bible that says, "These books are Sacred Scripture, and these aren't." So, why do they hold certain books to be sacred? Because of Tradition.

Remember, not everything Jesus said and did was written down. And even what was written down wasn't written down until decades after his death. By that point, the Church was already growing and spreading across the Roman Empire and beyond thanks to the preaching, teaching, and witness of the Apostles. These men handed on what they received from Jesus, and they expected their successors to do likewise.

Three times St.2 Paul included this very sentiment in his letters, writing, "I commend you because you remember me in everything and maintain the traditions even as I have delivered them to you" (1 Cor 11:2); "So then, brethren, stand firm and hold to the traditions which you were taught by us, either by word of mouth or by letter" (2 Thess 2:15); and "Now we command you, brethren, in the name of our Lord

Jesus Christ, that you keep away from any brother who is living in idleness and not in accord with the tradition that you received from us" (2 Thess 3:6).

So, Scripture itself tells us to hold fast to traditions, which have been handed down by word of mouth. It tells us to believe and live certain teachings that aren't included in Sacred Scripture. This, in large part, is because Scripture itself is part of Sacred Tradition. The reason we know which books are inspired by the Holy Spirit is because the Apostles and their successors handed down that knowledge, from generation to generation, until the Church decided it was prudent to officially compile that knowledge in a canon.

All that being said, all Catholic beliefs are supported by the Bible. Certain words or prayers or teachings may not be mentioned explicitly, but they all are mentioned at least implicitly. Sacred Scripture supports Sacred Tradition, just as Sacred Tradition supports Sacred Scripture.

Objection 2: Why Do Catholics Think They Need Tradition? Isn't Scripture Enough for Them?

Again, although Scripture is tremendously important to the Catholic Church and the life of its members, it is not the only way that God's Revelation has been passed down to us. Remember, St. John the Evangelist told us that there "are also many other things which Jesus did" and if they were all written out "the world itself could not contain the books that would be written" (John 21:25).

Likewise, before the Gospel of John is believed to have been written, the Church, not the documents of the Church, was named as the "pillar and bulwark of the truth" (1 Tim 3:15). The Church existed more than a generation before even the earliest epistles of the New Testament, and the term New Testament itself refers to the New Covenant, which specifically refers to the Eucharist and, therefore, the liturgy.

At the Last Supper, Jesus gave his disciples his Body and his Blood, specifically calling the offered chalice "the new covenant in my blood"

(Luke 22:20) and instructing us to "do this in remembrance" of him (Luke 22:19). The New Covenant, or Testament, was an action to be done before it was a book to be written down.

Moreover, Jesus didn't command his Apostles to write down the stories, accounts, and miracles. He commanded them to celebrate the Eucharist; baptize people in the name of Father, Son, and Holy Spirit; and make disciples of all nations. Writing the Gospel down helped the Apostles hand on the Tradition of the Church, but it wasn't the Tradition in full, just a part of it.

It's also important to note that this question usually arises in reference to the doctrine of *sola scriptura*, which means putting our faith in "Scripture alone." This idea, which is embraced by many groups of Protestants, is not found in Scripture. As mentioned above, Scripture itself tells us to hold fast to traditions and what we have heard. Scripture embraces the whole of Tradition and points us to the teaching authority of St. Peter and the other Apostles. *Sola scriptura* rejects that authority, which subsists in the Church's Magisterium, and ultimately that makes *sola scriptura* an unbiblical teaching contrary to Sacred Scripture.

Objection #3: The Catholic Church Added Books to Their Bible. How Can You Do That?

Catholic translations of the Bible have a total of seventy-three books (forty-six in the Old Testament and twenty-seven in the New Testament), while most translations embraced by Protestants have seven fewer books. The reason for this, in part, goes back to the Protestant Reformation. But in some ways it goes back even further, to the first centuries of the Church's life.

During those early years, most of the first Christian communities used the Septuagint, which is the Greek translation of the Old Testament. The Septuagint contained the forty-six books of the Old Testament that Catholics use today. The whole reason a Greek version of the Old Testament existed, however, was because of Hellenization, that is, the spread and eventual dominance of Greek and Roman culture across the Mediterranean world.

Not everyone thought Hellenization was a good thing, as they believed it was suppressing other cultural traditions, so, not surprisingly, there was pushback against it. Evidence suggests that part of that resistance was a rabbinical synod at Jamnia or Javneh. There, a group of Jewish rabbis decided that only those books that were originally written in, or existed in, Hebrew should be considered part of the Jewish Scriptures. That meant rejecting seven books that were written in Greek: Tobit, Judith, Wisdom, Sirach, Baruch, 1 Maccabees, and 2 Maccabees. It also meant rejecting certain passages in the books of Daniel and Esther.

After this decision was made, the early Christians continued using the Septuagint. They saw no need to change the version of the Old Testament they used, as they no longer followed the authority of the Jewish rabbis. Moreover, in the New Covenant the Church's Magisterium, not people who rejected the New Covenant, had the authority to determine which books were and weren't divinely inspired. Accordingly, for well over one thousand years the use of the Septuagint, with its seven "extra books," went virtually unquestioned.

During the sixteenth century the new Protestant "reformers" began questioning their use, primarily because these books referred to specific doctrines (e.g., praying for the dead) with which some reformers disagreed. Eventually, Protestants began using only those Old Testament books considered "canonical" by the Jewish rabbis, which is why their Bibles have fewer books than the Bibles used by Catholics.